READING PARADISE LOST

D1437559

Three Poets, in three distant Ages born,
Greece, Italy, and England did adorn.
The First in loftiness of thought Surpass'd,
The Next in Majesty; in both the Last.
The force of Nature cou'd no farther goe:
To make a Third she joynd the former two.

PAMELA WOOF

Reading
Paradise Lost

★

WITH ENGRAVINGS FROM
THE FIRST ILLUSTRATED
EDITION OF THE POEM
PUBLISHED IN 1688

THE WORDSWORTH TRUST
GRASMERE

First published 2004, reprinted 2005

ISBN 1 870787 93 5

Designed by Stephen Hebron
Set in 10 / 12 Adobe Bembo
Printed by Titus Wilson, Kendal

CONTENTS

Preface vii

Paradise Lost I

Book I 9
Book II 31
Book III 49
Book IV 63

Interlude 87

Book V 89
Book VI 101
Book VII 109
Book VIII 119
Book IX 131
Book X 155
Book XI 179
Book XII 197

A Note on the Illustrations

The engravings heading each chapter are taken from the first illustrated edition of *Paradise Lost*, published in folio by Jacob Tonson in 1688. They are after designs by John Baptist Medina, and Bernard Lens (Book IX). The frontispiece of Milton is after a portrait by William Faithorne. The verses are by John Dryden.

PREFACE

IN THE WINTER of 2003–4 I began to think about the need to bring *Paradise Lost* as a poem to people who might be coming to Grasmere to enjoy the exhibition, planned for summer 2004, on famous illustrations to *Paradise Lost*. I felt that people would enjoy the exhibition more if they were more familiar with the poem. I offered to write an essay; my intention was to help readers approach this perhaps formidable and yet most wonderful poem. The essay developed, and of course it cannot but be inadequate to encompass the magnificent and subtle resonances of Milton's language and ideas. The essay grew, and an 'Interlude' was written after Book IV, promising brevity; yet rightly or wrongly I felt it necessary to offer Milton's words rather than to summarise. Brevity gradually escaped.

The one thing that has not fluctuated is my enthusiasm for *Paradise Lost*. The poem is as great as I always knew it was, and I hope that my notes here will remind those who know the poem already of that greatness, and help those who are unfamiliar with it to enjoy this seventeenth-century masterpiece that is still a masterpiece. Milton's creation made from his own and his century's 'dark materials' (II, 916) has brought new inspiration to writers, readers, and play-goers of today; it is time to turn to Milton himself.

The rightness of mounting an exhibition on Milton at the Wordsworth Trust in Grasmere has become more and more apparent. Wordsworth indeed was 'the best knower of Milton', and in my own consideration of Milton in this place, it has seemed not inappropriate here and there to discuss aspects of Wordsworth's poetry that are close to Milton's. In bringing together the illustrations of *Paradise Lost* and a presentation of the artists who were inspired by the poem, I am one of many who must thank my husband Robert Woof, Director of the Wordsworth Trust. He has been the creator. And he has been especially kind in giving me the occasion to re-read and to write on this great poem. He has listened and commented, always well, as I have read sections to him. I would like also to thank Sally Woodhead for her superb assistance and patience in putting words on to a computer. And Stephen Hebron, as ever, and of course, for bringing a more than pleasing design to this reading of *Paradise Lost*.

I have used my old Alastair Fowler text of *Paradise Lost* in *The Poems of John Milton*, edited by John Carey and Alastair Fowler, Longmans Annotated English Poets, 1968, with some glances at the second edition of *Paradise Lost*, edited by Fowler, Longman, Pearson Education, 1998.

Grasmere
May 2004

PARADISE LOST

BUT WHY READ *Paradise Lost* now? Is it not enough to know the story, wonder at the marvellous illustrations and leave this poet quietly to our memories of school and college, to his fit audience of few admirers (relatively few) and perhaps to contemporary poets whose trade, like Milton's, is words. We could simply ignore the poem, but whatever our attitude, *Paradise Lost*, like Mont Blanc in Shelley's poem of that name, 'yet gleams on high'; it is distinctly there and in reading or re-reading it, we discover why we are reading it. There is no answer to the query, why read *Paradise Lost* now. The urgencies of the poem as we climb and move into its world provide for each reader certainties of poetic richness, now this one, now that, now two at once, now several, and soon there seems no need to ask the question at all. Readers, at a line or passage, may find themselves for or against the poet: no matter. We become caught up by Milton's passionate ideas, by a debate with a poem where ideas are deeply felt, where music and thinking are inextricable.

Despite the size of the endeavour, we have to try to interpret *Paradise Lost* for ourselves. Many of us are, after all, inheritors of a Northern Protestant ethic which assumes individual responsibility and the worth of each man's interpretation of God, scripture, the Church, the world and our purpose in it. Milton was writing a Protestant epic, and he offers strong and conflicting opinions for readers to sift through. We may or may not agree with the views of Blake, Byron, Shelley, Keats, John Clare, even Wordsworth and Coleridge as, magnetised by Milton, they variously absorbed, continued, argued with, rewrote bits of *Paradise Lost*; we may or may not see the poem's primary thrust as towards social revolution or Christian soul-making. Our abstract conclusions are less than the poem's significance. *Paradise Lost* is not theology or political argument or history; it is poetry.

Our pace in reading can be what we will; we might choose to struggle with passages that seem at first glance to be embedded in seventeenth-century learning or classical mythology or biblical history; we might leap from highlight to highlight as when first meeting a great opera. We might prefer the human characters, the frail, beautiful, imperfect Eve and her Adam whose disobedience we may not, in our complex of feeling, entirely lament. We may like to bring Milton's views into our present discussions of gender, the role of women, authority and the function of monarchy. We may enjoy pondering the place of Civil War politics in a poem based upon Genesis, or stay with the natural beauty of the Garden of Eden. We may be curious about Milton's Hell: is it a physical or a mental state, or both? Or about his angels: do they or do they not know what love, apart from the love of God, is? We may wonder how a believing poet can permit himself to put God into a fiction. The poem is a world to wander in, and with, without, or despite, some nudging from Milton, we can choose our several paths and our directions.

The Title and the Story

The whole poem is here in two words, 'Paradise Lost', which in their tension pull against each other: there was Paradise, and it was and is Lost. This is the story in little of the poem, and it is still our story: our desire for Paradise, our knowledge that we must lose it, and our sense, despite the loss, that we must ourselves strive to create a different Paradise, arguably a better one.

Those two words 'Paradise' and 'Lost' reverberate, and the poem takes twelve books to tell the well-known Genesis account of the creation of the world, the creation of Adam and Eve, of the Garden of Eden, of the prohibition concerning the fruit of the Tree of Knowledge, of the temptation of Eve by the serpent, the temptation of Adam by Eve, the punishment, the expulsion from the Garden. Like all epic poets, Milton takes a familiar story; no-one reads this poem to find out in a hurried kind of way what happens; rather to ponder on why it has to happen.

Milton tidied up the plot, finding or introducing a psychological coherence out of far-flung biblical verses: in Genesis a creature, a mere serpent, persuades Eve to taste the fruit, while later, books ahead in Isaiah, we read the lament:

> How art thou fall'n from heaven, O Lucifer, son of the morning! how art thou cut down to the ground ...

Ahead again, in Revelation we are told that

> There was war in heaven: Michael and his angels fought against the dragon: and the dragon fought and his angels. And prevailed not; neither was their place found any more in heaven. And the great dragon was cast out, that old serpent, called the Devil, and Satan, which deceiveth the whole world; he was cast out into the earth, and his angels were cast out with him. (Revelation, 12: 7–9)

For Milton, the dragon/serpent/Devil had been the great light-bearing Archangel Lucifer, and it is he, a new composite character, Lucifer/Satan/serpent, who makes the bid to tempt and destroy God's recent and favoured creation Man. Satan, Milton suggests, does this in revenge for his own and his rebel angels' expulsion from heaven after their doomed challenge to God's supremacy, after their fight, defeat and fall into hell. The story was so well-known, and it still is, even with Milton's addition of that first angelic fall so seamlessly bound into Adam and Eve's story, that the poet, like his classical epic forebears, had no need to re-tell it in a chronological order of events. He moves up and down the story dramatically as film-makers do, with flashes backwards and forwards.

[3]

The Beginning

No beginning could be grander:

> Of man's first disobedience, and the fruit
> Of that forbidden tree, whose mortal taste
> Brought death into the world, and all our woe,
> With loss of Eden, till one greater man
> Restore us, and regain the blissful seat,
> Sing heavenly Muse ... (I, 1–6)

The monosyllables of those first lines beat out the dreadful significance of the subject; the contrasting polysyllable 'disobedience', heavy, like the word 'forbidden', with disapproval, takes us into a moral punitive world of death which continues from that first disobedience up to the present and includes all our woe and the woe to come. It is this weight of universal history rather than the hope of redemption that sounds the first note – and it is a dark note – of the poem, and it is this that Milton begs his heavenly Muse to sing.

The fall of a great civilised city, Troy in *The Iliad*, the testing dangers of Odysseus's ten-year journey home to Ithaca, the emotional as well as the chance hardships of Aeneas as he fulfilled the gods' bidding to establish Rome, these had been the subjects of epic for Homer and Virgil. Milton's subject was bigger, and in his view more important as it was emphatically spiritual rather than primarily political or national. Only Dante had had a comparable poetic ambition, making himself in *The Divine Comedy* his own central character who must undergo an exploration of Hell, Purgatory and Heaven for the soul's salvation, the soul of Everyman as well as Dante's own. But *The Divine Comedy* was an Italian, early fourteenth-century Catholic work. Milton's epic is Protestant and it was for the English; he had considered writing in Latin, and would have achieved in that language a wide and cultivated European readership. As it was, his heroic poem was for the England of his own time and of the future.

He recognised the size of his ambition and in the continuing lines of his very long first sentence he discusses his aim. In that single sentence at the poem's start both the subject and the poet are introduced to the reader. The poet is introduced via the Muse whom he begs to help him:

> Sing heavenly Muse, that on the secret top
> Of Oreb, or of Sinai, didst inspire
> That shepherd, who first taught the chosen seed,
> In the beginning how the heavens and earth
> Rose out of chaos: or if Sion hill
> Delight thee more, and Siloa's brook that flowed
> Fast by the oracle of God; I thence
> Invoke thy aid to my advent'rous song,
> That with no middle flight intends to soar
> Above the Aonian mount, while it pursues
> Things unattempted yet in prose or rhyme. (I, 6–16)

The difficult sentence of sixteen lines thus ends with breath-taking ambition before, almost without stopping, and taking breath for a further ten lines, the next sentence defines more closely the massive aim of the poet and his massive subject.

Meanwhile this invocation to the heavenly Muse might well be an obstacle to readers of today at the very outset of what is to be an extraordinarily simple poem. The poem's first five lines of mainly plain immediate words give way here, in line 6, to a more decorated style; though tending to Puritanism, Milton had leanings towards the baroque, that style, in painting, of swirling elaborate grandeur and ornate detail, that he knew from the paintings and architecture he had seen in Italy. Here, in language, his single sentence continues to wind its syntax through interwoven clauses and its vast subject matter ranges over time and space until the personal 'I' of the author finally confronts his audacious task,

> Things unattempted yet in prose or rhyme.

The grandest of all Muses is invoked, the divine Muse, nothing less. And Milton does not see a response as an impossibility, for that same Muse had once before inspired a shepherd, the shepherd who went to the tops of mountains, to Mount Horeb, and Mount Sinai, and heard from out of cloud, fire and smoke, the voice of God. That shepherd became the teacher of the chosen people, the Children of Israel, and among other things he told them about the creation of the world: Moses was that shepherd and Moses, Milton believed, was the writer of the Book of Genesis, the very basis of Milton's poem. And Milton, too, in accepted pastoral tradition, had written of himself as a poet-shepherd in his early elegy *Lycidas*, a poem that explored as one of its subjects the writing of poetry in a flawed and fallen world; now, in *Paradise Lost*, he was ready to teach the modern chosen people, the imperfect English nation, and in part what he will teach is what Moses had taught, the story of what happened 'In the beginning', the creation of the world.

With vast strides Milton moves in that first sentence from the Creation and the early haunts of the heavenly Muse on the mountains of the Old Testament to those of the New; the Muse might now be found about Mount Zion and the nearby pool of Siloam near Calvary, the pool whose waters under the direction of Christ had brought sight to a blind disciple. We must remember as we jump forward into the poet's own times that Milton himself was blind during the writing of *Paradise Lost*, and is, in this address to the heavenly Muse, asking for inner sight, for insight. He ends the sentence stressing his need for help in composing a song so 'advent'rous'; this song is the whole of *Paradise Lost*. He will fly to heights yet unknown, reaching far above the Aeonian Mount, the classical mountain of the Muses, Mount Helicon with its own local spring of inspiration. We are back again with Milton's ambition to place himself not only on a par with Homer and Virgil, but, in the service of his greater subject, upon a height beyond them.

High fliers, of course, may fall, as did Icarus, as does, in this poem disastrously, Lucifer who becomes Satan, as do Adam and Eve. Milton knows the danger, and appeals in the last lines of this first paragraph not even to the divine Muse, the heavenly Muse, but directly to God himself in his manifestation as the Holy Spirit:

[6]

> And chiefly thou O Spirit, that dost prefer
> Before all temples the upright heart and pure,
> Instruct me, for thou knowst; thou from the first
> Wast present, and with mighty wings outspread
> Dove-like satst brooding on the vast abyss
> And mad'st it pregnant: what in me is dark
> Illumine, what is low raise and support;
> That to the highth of this great argument
> I may assert eternal providence,
> And justify the ways of God to men. (I, 17–26)

And where – for the thinking Puritan – is the Holy Spirit most likely to be found but in the believing heart of the Christian, a temple more treasured by Milton's God than any building. And so again the poet returns to the creation of the world, to beginnings, to origins, for the Holy Spirit was there from the first, when the heavens and earth rose out of chaos. It is Milton's hope that the Spirit will be there now for him, the poet, inspiring him at the beginning of this poem. The creation of the poem, Milton implies, is as great a creative act as the creation of the world. The same powers are needed for both, God's powers. Milton declares his need with humility: 'what in me is dark / Illumine, what is low raise and support', and then comes the stupendous grandeur of his ambition: to

> assert eternal providence,
> And justify the ways of God to men.

The reader will decide by the end of the poem whether or not Milton has succeeded and whether or not success or failure matters.

With this first paragraph the story begins. Though complex, the paragraph provides the necessary overture to the symphonic musical organisation of *Paradise Lost* and, of course, if the reader simply reads these first twenty-six lines aloud, the essential meaning will be communicated without any such pointers as these foregoing explanatory remarks.

BOOK I

IT WAS NO use looking at history to justify God's ways. God was inscrutable. He had seemed from 1640 to encourage the anti-bishop, anti-monarchal rebellion with the Roundhead victories of the Civil War and the establishment of the Commonwealth; but with Cromwell's death in 1658, with divisions within the reforming party, and with the Restoration of Charles II in 1660, it struck Puritans that God was abandoning his saints to the moral anarchy of history. Milton was composing most of *Paradise Lost* at a time when all he had fought for politically was in the process of being reversed. Nevertheless, he keeps faith and tries to exonerate God, beginning in Book I with Lucifer/ Satan, the brilliant rebel against authority. Milton himself had rebelled against authority, against monarchy. He detested absolute rule; Satan had lost, as the English Revolution had lost. We have admiration for the fallen archangel even on the basis of his loss, as we admire any hero and brave loser who fights insuperable odds. In Book I we meet Satan and the fallen angels already defeated and hurled out of heaven, prostrate upon the burning lake of Hell. Neither Satan's courage nor his rhetoric deserts him:

> What though the field be lost?
> All is not lost; the unconquerable will ... (I, 105–6)

but then the next line brings in another note:

> And study of revenge, immortal hate ... (I, 107)

Do we not find sympathy more difficult here? 'study of revenge'? Yet while this is hard for our liberal moral consciousness to take, the next lines,

> And courage never to submit or yield
> And what is else not to be overcome? (I, 108–9)

in their single-minded declaration restore Satan to the status of hero. He begins to fascinate as he develops an inner life; we recognise human complexity. 'Vaunting aloud', he tries not to discourage his nearest companion, but Milton tells us that within he is 'racked with deep despair' (126). He allows himself briefly the luxury of lament:

> Is this the region, this the soil, the clime,
> Said then the lost archangel, this the seat
> That we must change for heaven, this mournful gloom
> For that celestial light? Be it so ...
> > Farewell happy fields
> Where joy forever dwells: hail horrors, hail ... (I, 242–50)

The loss of 'celestial light' is deeply felt, and some of its despair seeps into later literature, into Wordsworth's loss, for example, as, mystified, he expresses his own sad knowledge in 1802 that for him too the celestial light has changed:

> There was a time when meadow, grove and stream,
> > The earth and every common sight,
> > > To me did seem
> > > > Apparelled in celestial light,
> The glory and the freshness of a dream.
> > ('Ode, Intimations of Immortality', 1–5)

The lost archangel of course swings fast into at least an appearance of recovery, almost converting defeat into victory, for he brings, he declares,

> A mind not to be changed by place or time.
> The mind is its own place, and in itself
> Can make a heaven of hell, a hell of heaven... .
> > Here at least
> We shall be free ... (I, 253–9)

'Man's unconquerable mind' of Wordsworth's sonnet lies some hundred and fifty years ahead, as well as Byron's and Shelley's studies of the mind's reactions to imprisonment and their pæans to Liberty (for example, *The Prisoner of Chillon*, *The Lament of*

Tasso, Prometheus Unbound); but surely all man's Protestant and humanist dignity rises to applaud Satan's words. Not surprisingly many readers, Blake amongst them, have declared that Milton was of the devil's party without knowing it. The mind's pre-eminence and its power to overcome surroundings is a fine uplifting thought and we admire Satan; yet even here there is a smack of Faustian arrogance, as Satan continues with ideas of ambition and rule:

> Here we may reign secure, and in my choice
> To reign is worth ambition though in hell:
> Better to reign in hell than serve in heaven. (I, 261–3)

In this speech as a whole Satan has slipped from the inclusive pronoun 'we' to the egotistic 'I' before moving diplomatically back again, and it becomes clear that there will ever be only one leader in hell, Satan. The forceful single-line epigram, 'Better to reign in hell than serve in heaven' tells us at the speech's climax that Satan, formerly Lucifer the great archangel, rebelled against God's authority, not in the cause of democratic liberty, but to replace it with his own control. Yet a certain nobility remains Satan's throughout Book I; his very presence is magnificent:

> He above the rest
> In shape and gesture proudly eminent
> Stood like a tower; his form had yet not lost
> All her original brightness, nor appeared
> Less than archangel ruined, and the excess
> Of glory obscured: as when the sun new risen
> Looks through the horizontal misty air
> Shorn of his beams ... (I, 589–96)

The beauty of the sun new risen in connection with Satan must recall for us Isaiah's elegiac, 'How art thou fall'n from heaven, O Lucifer, son of the morning', yet the misty air and the shorn beams tell us that glorious Lucifer is even now darkening into Satan. There can be no sun in hell and Satan is associated with light for the last time here, and here, only in a simile which goes on to compare his ruined brightness to the 'disastrous twilight' of the moon in 'dim eclipse'; thus the simile carries with it a seventeenth-century fear of omens that threaten catastrophe. It carried too, more precisely, what was seen as a suspiciously subversive thrust by Milton against the King, for the monarch's symbol was traditionally the shining sun; a sun shorn of its beams, even as an image, could hint at further rebellion.

As Satan prepares to speak to his followers, 'Millions of spirits',

> condemned
> For ever now to have their lot in pain, ...
> For his fault amerced
> Of heaven, and from eternal splendours flung
> For his revolt, (I, 607–11)

he is moved at the thought of their loss and at their loyalty:

> faithful how they stood
> Their glory withered. (I, 611–12)

His heart not yet hardened, he breaks down before he can speak:

> Thrice he essayed, and thrice in spite of scorn,
> Tears such as angels weep, burst forth ... (I, 619–20)

The grief makes him human; it is the grief at failure of those who, like Satan, lead aggressive and violent attempts to change history. Their actions do in ways unlooked-for change some things and what they create cannot be undone; history cannot be reversed, and before Satan turns to the only direction he can now have, that of revenge, he weeps, perhaps for the sheer inevitable failure of the attempt. The tears are angel's tears and we sense their intensity of despair since angels were thought not to shed tears at all. How different from the tears at the end of the poem; Adam and Eve for their disobedience are exiled from Paradise:

> Some natural tears they dropped, but wiped them soon;
> The world was all before them ...

Fully human, they wipe their human tears and go towards their future lives in time where regret and hope are ambiguously mingled.

Before turning to God, and to Adam and Eve, we might dwell a little longer on Satan and Book I, which is, after all, the gateway to the poem. Milton, as we have seen, gives Satan a grandeur of presence, a brilliant rhetoric, a real anguish of feeling and great courage. Magnificence has to be given him for God himself would be diminished if his adversary were a mere pawn easily dismissed, or a force for evil so totally recognisable as to be universally rejected. Milton is writing on a knife's edge at the beginning of his poem: the reader must sympathise with Satan, must admire him, and simultaneously must move to condemnation. The poet prepares the reader: before we meet Satan and are ourselves seduced by the 'archangel ruin'd', we are provided with pointers that place him firmly at a moral low: 'foul revolt', 'The infernal serpent', 'guile', 'envy and revenge', 'deceived', 'pride', 'aspiring', 'ambitious', 'impious war', 'vain attempt'. Only when we have assimilated the narrator's judgment here (I, 32–44) can Milton with any safety make his fallen rebel interesting. First, he turns him into an object and he does this by making use of a Latinate syntax. He begins a sentence with its grammatical object – him, Satan:

> Him the almighty power
> Hurled headlong flaming from the ethereal sky
> With hideous ruin and combustion down
> To bottomless perdition, there to dwell
> In adamantine chains and penal fire,
> Who durst defy the omnipotent to arms.
> Nine times the space that measures day and night
> To mortal men, he with his horrid crew
> Lay vanquished, rolling in the fiery gulf
> Confounded though immortal ... (I, 44–53)

[13]

A sense of physical falling, an upside-downness, is reflected in the inverted word-order. And it is no gentle fall: 'Hurled headlong flaming' is planted with huge force at a line's beginning, and immediately after its object, 'Him', and the hurling subject, 'the almighty power'. Line after line then continues seamlessly dropping without a pause over the line-endings like the fall itself. Satan is no active charismatic leader here; he is passive, subject to a poet's grammar and subject to cosmic time and space in a literal fall to a literal hell. Milton is close enough to the popular medieval imagination about hell to make the place physical as well as a never-ending pain of mind. It is a dungeon that 'As one great furnace flamed', and just as we begin here to create out of this furnace a brilliance of light, all is extinguished, for

> from those flames
> No light, but rather darkness visible
> Served only to discover sights of woe ... (I, 62–4)

The possibility of light has simply intensified the darkness, and darkness itself paradoxically reveals 'sights'. The scene is a confusion of disintegrating opposites – light and dark, and good qualities immediately negatived in

> doleful shades, where peace
> And rest can never dwell, hope never comes
> That comes to all ... (I, 65–7)

We perhaps begin to sense as we read Book I how happy was Milton's decision to begin his epic so far into the story. The war preceding the angels' fall will come later; here it has a mere mention; what is stressed is a Fall. What will happen, we know, is another Fall. There are differences, but the Falls are alike in that they result in qualities and conditions that must, like darkness and light, exist in conflict, in paradox. An archangel fallen has a nobility though this is yoked with destructive impulse. Satan, writ large, is a version of fallen man; he sounds the note of the poem at its start, the note indeed of most literature about man,

in action how like an angel, in apprehension how like a
god – the beauty of the world, the paragon of animals!
And yet to me what is this quintessence of dust?

Hamlet, thinking thus, had no hope; Milton has, and this is
explored in the great difference between the Fall of Satan and
the Fall of Man. Meanwhile the theme is grandly begun in
Book I.

Constantly Milton stresses Satan's power and constantly in
his language he undermines it; it is 'the superior fiend', not the
ruined archangel, who 'was moving toward the shore' (284) and
whose mighty physical presence can then, but only after we
have accepted 'fiend', be described admiringly: his very shield
'Hung on his shoulders like the moon' (287), his great spear,

> to equal which the tallest pine
> Hewn on Norweyan hills, to be the mast
> On some great ammiral, were but a wand,
> He walked with … (I, 292–5)

Here Milton presents the magnified figure of some heroic figure out of epic: the shield of Homer's Achilles for instance was
seen in relation to the bountiful earth, for it had depicted on
it scenes of man's fundamental activities upon the land; Satan's
shield is linked not to earth but to the moon,

> whose orb
> Through optic glass the Tuscan artist views
> At evening … (I, 288–90)

It is the surface of the moon as seen by Galileo, 'the Tuscan
artist', that excites Milton. He had himself, it is thought, visited
the troubled, blind and excommunicated scientist at his house
near Florence. It is some measure of Milton's respect for Satan
that he can associate him with the new discoveries, not with
the old limited universe, earth-centred or sun-centred, but with
a universe that is boundless, infinite, and which, for Milton,
served not to threaten but to expand dynamically our vision
of the divine. At the same time there is some undermining of

Satan and his shield; the moon has not the stable presence of either the earth or the unchanging heavenly bodies above the moon; nor has it any essential light; the glory of its waning and waxing is borrowed. Neither does Satan's spear have entirely positive or mighty associations. A ship's mast in epic tradition gave dignity to a weapon, but a pine tree, even 'the tallest pine', is less straightforward and has undertones of savage brutality: it was the trunk of a pine that the one-eyed giant, the Cyclops Polyphemus, used to walk with after Odysseus blinded him following the giant's hideous slaughter and gluttonous eating of almost all of Odysseus's men. Altogether, Milton's passage carries mingled messages: that Satan is habited like a warrior is proper because he has fallen directly from the battlefield in Heaven on to the 'burning marl' of Hell, but, of course, it is a criticism too. Milton will make this clear as the poem grows; Satan is already out of date in assuming that power struggles between good and evil will be fought on any battlefield or be won or lost through any show of military might. It is a lesson we still learn. Significantly too, Satan, despite his immortal and heroic physique, can now feel pain; now, even like Polyphemus, or any of us in infirmity or age, he has to have a walking stick and he uses his great spear

> to support uneasy steps
> Over the burning marl. (I, 295–6)

There is an insecurity here. Indeed, a sense of insecurity pervades *Paradise Lost*; fallen man, like this archangel fallen and new to his changed conditions, will be constantly insecure. *Paradise Lost* is like a dream poem, and its readers, like its characters, are always on the move into new spaces never before encountered, new problems for the first time discussed. We have no security even in the beautiful recognisable world of the Garden, for we know that it cannot last.

Yet Satan carries on, despite the pain and the strangeness of his new experience, despite his uneasy steps (and how much might Milton, a blind poet, himself walking with difficulty, feel with Satan in this homely aspect of his own predicament).

[16]

Satan carries on:

> Natheless he so endured, till on the beach
> Of that inflamèd sea, he stood and called
> His legions, angel forms, who lay entranced
> Thick as autumnal leaves that strew the brooks
> In Vallombrosa, where th'Etrurian shades
> High overarched embower ... (I, 299–304)

His courage admits no question, and, in Milton's description of the seemingly enchanted multitudes of angels, we are granted some respite from the burning and the torrid clime; there is a coolness about the brooks of the simile and the shadowy places underneath the trees. This is a relief, but, at the same time, we cannot forget that fallen leaves are used by Homer, Virgil and Dante to indicate the huge numbers of dead that roam their underworlds. Milton's angels too are dead, though immortal; they are dead to goodness. Likewise the Tuscan valley, Vallombrosa, that the poet chooses for his leaves, with its literal meaning of 'valley' and 'shadows', comes close, despite, perhaps because of, its seductive sound 'Vallombrosa', to the valley of the shadow of death of Psalm 23. None of these associations augur well for the fallen angels, and their plight continues less than happy in Milton's further simile of their likeness to sedge or reeds, helplessly 'afloat' on the Red Sea along with the 'floating carcases / And broken chariot wheels' of Pharoah and his Memphian chivalry destroyed by God's intervention as 'they pursued / The sojourners of Goshen', the Children of Israel, across the Red Sea.

Similes can thus add nuances, indeed often more than one, and sometimes conflicting nuances, to a situation in the poem; and if the reader recognises or searches out the stories in the similes, there is simply more there to think about as the layers of meaning underneath the surface meaning contribute their own flavours to the main narrative. If we do not know the stories in the similes, we still take the main thrust of them and appreciate their difference from the narrative. Similes have their value even as they carry the reader out of the poem's strange imagined almost surreal worlds and into the temporary comfort of the familiar.

Satan addresses the angels 'abject and lost' and uses their former titles, as though by words he can disguise from them their state of total defeat; as though, if they would make an effort, heaven could be retrieved:

> Princes, potentates,
> Warriors, the flower of heaven, once yours, now lost,
> If such astonishment as this can seize
> Eternal spirits; or have ye chosen this place
> After the toil of battle to repose
> Your wearied virtue, for the ease you find
> To slumber here, as in the vales of heaven? (I, 315–21)

It is all unreal, purely political; it is mere language; the rebel angels' titles were potent only while they had loyalty to God; they can now have no virtue, wearied or otherwise. But the grim humour of Satan, like that of some superior officer, shames them into military order. He commands them:

> Awake, arise or be for ever fall'n. (I, 330)

In the larger sense they are of course for ever fallen, but, like ordinary wearied fighting men throughout history, they respond to the soldierly language:

> They heard, and were abashed, and up they sprung
> Upon the wing, as when men wont to watch
> On duty, sleeping found by whom they dread,
> Rouse and bestir themselves ere well awake. (I, 331–4)

The speed of their response lies in the three main verbs in the first line here, joined by 'and', and placed in contrast with the rest of the sentence with its more complex syntax and its hint that the angels' obedience to Satan springs less from love than from fear. Their predicament is corroborated by the double negatives of the next lines, where their pain of both mind and body forces itself into recognition:

[18]

> Nor did they not perceive the evil plight
> In which they were, or the fierce pains not feel ... (I, 335–6)

This double negative construction perhaps allows the reader to play fleetingly with the idea that these angels, who after all are rather like ordinary soldiers found sleeping on duty, might just have escaped the pain; but they have not; nor have they, mere followers and foot-soldiers as they are, really understood the moral as well as the physical dimension of their situation, their 'evil plight'. The word 'evil' in connection with Satan has a force they have not so far begun to understand.

The angels assemble and they are as numberless (and will later be as persistent in plaguing humanity) as the locusts that 'darkened all the land of Nile' (343), and again we are, through a simile, in a historical situation where God, via Moses, intervenes to protect the Chosen People from an 'impious Pharaoh'. On the heels of these lines condemning a monarch as 'impious', Milton refers to Satan as the 'great sultan' (348) with all that phrase's overtones for Milton and his readers of barbaric splendour and Turkish cruelty. The similes rise in power and the fallen angels now are as many, as anonymous and as frightening as the Goths and Vandals, those 'barbarous sons' from 'the populous north', who 'Came like a deluge on the south' (351–4)), and destroyed a civilisation.

The next section of Book I takes us away from the immediate narrative and into the future names and activities of the twelve leading angels whom Satan chooses as his council; the reader sees here a parody of Christ and his disciples. We are not told what names these angels had had in heaven; their action has wiped out their identities. We know only Satan's original name, 'Lucifer'; for the rest,

> of their names in heavenly records now
> Be no memorial blotted out and razed
> By their rebellion, from the books of life. (I, 361–3)

The narrator is calm and the condemnation is final. The catalogue of fallen angels identifies them in their future manifestations as pagan gods. In place of a Homeric catalogue of ships, Milton offers brief story after brief story to characterise western civilisation's idolatrous religions. The passage (381–522) is thick with the names of places, of gods and of pagan practices; it is choked with Semitic, Egyptian, Greek, Roman, Celtic folklore and mythology; its turgid grandeur of style is a sign perhaps of the very falseness of its content. At times Milton's anger against religious abomination spills over into anger against, say, Charles I:

> First Moloch, horrid king besmeared with blood
> Of human sacrifice and parents' tears,
> Though for the noise of drums and timbrels loud
> Their children's cries unheard, that passed through fire
> To his grim idol. (I, 392–6)

King Charles I, in Milton's view, was similarly a 'horrid king besmeared with blood'; his cowardly complicity in the death of the Earl of Strafford, for instance, had 'plunged him all over' in a 'sea of innocent blood' (Milton's pamphlet, *Eikonoklastes*, 1649, Chapter II); he had been responsible for other deaths and, like kings generally, surrounded himself with deceiving ritual noise and fanfares. Before moving on from Moloch to Baal and the moon-goddess Ashtoreth, it is a relief to come upon a single plain line in praise of Josiah who was given, according to the Book of Kings, to zealously expelling idolatrous priests and beating down and breaking the altars and images of false gods. These gods had gained a wide following

> Till good Josiah drove them thence to hell. (I, 418)

'Good Josiah' of course was rather a favourite with the reforming Puritans who had their own iconoclastic agenda.

As Moloch is the first of the fallen angels/pagan gods in the list, Belial comes almost last,

than whom a spirit more lewd
Fell not from heaven, or more gross to love
Vice for itself. (I, 490–2)

Belial has no temples; his devotees are everywhere where hedonism and materialism dominate. Milton moves to the present tense as he discusses the continuing ascendancy of Belial with the implication of his hold on Restoration London:

In courts and palaces he also reigns
And in luxurious cities where the noise
Of riot ascends above their loftiest towers,
And injury and outrage: and when night
Darkens the streets, then wander forth the sons
Of Belial, flown with insolence and wine. (I, 497–502)

Theatres had re-opened after the restrictions of the Commonwealth and the new Cavalier court welcomed splendour; Milton, though he was no longer in danger of execution after the end of summer 1660, was humiliated by the changes, and he had every reason to fear and condemn the city maraudings of the sons of Belial.

Finally in the list come the gods who

on the snowy top
Of cold Olympus ruled the middle air
Their highest heaven ... (I, 515–7)

gods from a civilisation that Milton loved and had known from his earliest reading, the gods of Greece. But they were not true; their rule extended only to the middle air, and so these too, beginning as fallen angels, attended Satan's call along with those who would become brutish gods:

All these and more came flocking; but with looks
Down cast and damp, yet such wherein appeared
Obscure some glimpse of joy, to have found their chief
Not in despair, to have found themselves not lost
In loss itself ... (I, 522–526)

[21]

They cannot fully see their loss and Satan of course is in despair, but that obscure glimpse of joy at finding their leader is touching and Satan responds; he

> gently raised
> Their fainting courage, and dispelled their fears. (I, 529–30)

It is the act of a great commander, but Milton reminds his readers of the need to exercise judgment by telling us that the words Satan used were

> high words, that bore
> Semblance of worth, not substance. (I, 528–9)

Before we are given Satan's words directly, we witness how a huge defeated army like the one that fell with Satan can be exalted into feeling a solidarity, even a hope. Satan commands, and the sounds and signs of military order appear. To 'trumpets loud and clarions', Satan's mighty standard is 'upreared' and 'full high advanced'; it

> Shone like a meteor streaming to the wind
> With gems and golden lustre rich imblazed,
> Seraphic arms and trophies. (I, 537–9)

At this the 'universal host upsent / A shout that tore hell's concave' (541–2). It is a stirring scene. 'Ten thousand banners rise into the air', and the language continues to reflect upward movements and a corresponding rise in spirits. A softer music completes the military show and the angels move, united

> In perfect phalanx to the Dorian mood
> Of flutes and soft recorders; such as raised
> To highth of noblest temper heroes old
> Arming to battle … (I, 550–3)

The music, remarks Milton, is such as could assuage

> troubled thoughts, and chase
> Anguish and doubt and fear and sorrow and pain
> From mortal or immortal minds. (I, 557–9)

[22]

As the angels in perfect discipline move to the music, themselves now 'unmoved / With dread of death to flight or foul retreat', they find that the sound charms also

> Their painful steps o'er the burnt soil ... (I, 562)

It is a tribute to the power of music, and it is given to fallen angels in hell, whose pain and their efforts to overcome it seem to remind Milton of the 'troubled thoughts' of man, and man's

> Anguish and doubt and fear and sorrow and pain ...

This line, where mental troubles mount simply and inexorably, is stark and compelling; some hundred and fifty years later it could have been in Wordsworth's head when he spelled out the troubles that might come in the future to his sister:

> If solitude, or fear, or pain, or grief
> Should be thy portion ...
> > ('Tintern Abbey', 144–5)

If such should be her portion, she might combat trouble, Wordsworth suggests, by recalling the strength which he had received from nature, a strength that she herself might continue to receive:

> Therefore let the moon
> Shine on thee in thy solitary walk ...
> > ('Tintern Abbey', 135–6)

How different is Milton's seventeenth-century solace from that of Wordsworth, a poet of the Romantic period; for Milton the comfort is music, not nature, and it is most needed when angel or man has fallen and is suffering. We begin to perceive hints of a theme that will be explored in the poem: that the creative arts are part of man's consolation for the loss of Paradise.

Milton gives Satan a military company greater than any that has been known in history and of course the poet has to come out of hell and into history to indicate the comparative feebleness of such celebrated human armies as fought at Troy or Thebes or with Charlemagne. Satan's 'heart / Distends with pride' (571–2), and though moved, even to tears, as we have seen, he addresses his angels, and sums up the strife with 'the almighty' (ironically using that supreme title) as 'not inglorious, though the event was dire' (624); 'he who reigns / Monarch in heaven' had concealed his strength, asserts Satan, 'Which tempted our attempt'. For all his wit and his pride in military might, he moves away from the notion of another military encounter, speaks of the new created world and its possibly favoured inhabitants and slips in ideas that depend on deviousness,

> To work in close design, by fraud or guile ... (I, 646)

'to pry' (655), 'War / Open or understood must be resolved' (661–2). It is the strategy of cold war.

And it is less than heroic, but the angels, fired now by their own show of strength and the palpable magnetism of their leader, are one with him in continued defiance of that other

> who reigns
> Monarch in heaven ...
>   Upheld by old repute,
> Consent or custom ... (I, 637–40)

This presentation of God naturally inflames Satan's followers in their determination to continue in rebellion; the issues were real. Why, after all, had the Civil War been fought if not to change a monarchy upheld by 'old repute, consent or custom', if not to move English society to republicanism? Book I, however, with Satan at its centre, is hardly the place for Milton to demonstrate his conviction that the basis for monarchy in heaven is entirely different from that which Satan describes, and which prevailed on earth. The fallen angels absorb their leader's rhetoric; they want war and

>   out flew
> Millions of flaming swords, drawn from the thighs
> Of mighty cherubim; the sudden blaze

Far round illumined hell; highly they raged
Against the highest ... (I, 663–7)

Milton enjoys word-play as in the last lines here, like any seventeenth-century poet, and then allows his readers to enjoy a kind of devils' magic for the rest of Book I. The sense of unity and purpose that Satan has awakened is turned by the fallen angels into harmonious team-work as they, 'with wondrous art', place upon that fearful landscape a building, a court with debating chamber magnificent enough for Satan and his great compeers. It is Mammon naturally who knows where to find the building materials; even in heaven, comments Milton, Mammon had more admired

The riches of heaven's pavement, trodden gold,
Than aught divine or holy... (I, 681–3)

Thus, Mammon starts out on his path to sin, giving first place to the thing created rather than to the Creator. Mammon leads a brigade to a hill and they dig out 'ribs of gold'. 'Let none admire', comments Milton,

That riches grow in hell; that soil may best
Deserve the precious bane. (I, 690–2)

The now famous phrase, 'precious bane', is a tiny detail in the texture of this poem which is full of both big and little oppositions: the precious and the poisonous, light and dark, movements up and movements down, thoughts of liberty and of bondage, innocence and experience, death and life, evil and good. Here, the thought of digging out the precious bane gives Milton the opportunity to comment critically on contemporary materialism, for men too had been taught by Mammon, and have

Ransacked the centre, and with impious hands
Rifled the bowels of their mother earth
For treasures better hid. (I, 686–8)

With energy, with skill and with of course angelic art, or should we now define the art as devilish,

> out of the earth a fabric huge
> Rose like an exhalation ... (I, 710–11)

This is Pandaemonium, Milton's word for the seat of all spirits, or rather of all devilish spirits. A building rising like a breath from that soil of hell augurs little good, for vapoury exhalations from the earth were thought to warn of disaster, and of course were themselves insubstantial, illusory. Like a great stage device such as the most lavish masque created by Inigo Jones might faintly figure, Pandaemonium rose to the sound of music, to 'dulcet symphonies and voices sweet'. The theatrical aspect of Satan's rule, the pomp, the magnificent military show that drew his followers together, the glories of palatial building, all these are aspects of earthly kingship, and all these were much in evidence when Charles II entered London in May 1660; all these are placed in Milton's hell. It is perhaps significant that in Paradise there is no architecture, and unfallen man lives in a garden. Pandaemonium, with its Doric pillars, its golden architrave, its sculptures, its roof of fretted gold, its great brazen doors, is grander than any of the glorious pagan temples that Milton mentions for comparison, and if it reminds its readers of the still new St Peter's in Rome, that would not be amiss, for Milton considered such Catholic building as extravagant and unseemly for Christians seeking humility.

Yet it would seem, perhaps despite himself, that Milton took pleasure in the architecture of Pandaemonium; he gives it music to rise to. Troy itself, it is said, had been built to music, and theories in the Renaissance promoted the idea that musical proportions governed architecture. However that may be, Milton turns to discuss the architect and this allows both him and the reader briefly to leave the ingenious but artificial lighting of Pandaemonium by naphtha and asphaltus (pitch), and stay for a long day, albeit a sad one, in the sunshine of Greece. Before the architect's fall he had been known

In heaven by many a towered structure high (I, 733)

He was nameless now in hell; later in Italy,

> Men called him Mulciber; and how he fell
> From heaven, they fabled, thrown by angry Jove
> Sheer o'er the crystal battlements; from morn
> To noon he fell, from noon to dewy eve,
> A summer's day; and with the setting sun
> Dropped from the zenith like a falling star,
> On Lemnos the Aegaean isle; thus they relate,
> Erring; for he with this rebellious rout
> Fell long before; nor aught availed him now
> To have built in heaven high towers; nor did he scape
> By all his engines, but was headlong sent
> With his industrious crew to build in hell. (I, 740–51)

Milton here re-tells Homer's story (*Iliad*, I, 591–5) of the fall of Hephaestos (the Greek name for Vulcan or Mulciber). We seem to look down from the crystal battlements as we watch his fall, and we are with him during the great distance of his falling that takes the time of each section of a lengthening summer's day. By the time of the setting sun we have changed position and are on Lemnos looking upwards and watching him as he drops from the highest point of the heavens like a falling star; and it has taken until night. Milton's sentence has a continuousness like the fall itself and it moves remorselessly from heaven as far as hell at its close. The long fall through the sunshine has such an attractiveness at this point in the story of hell, that one wonders whether the poet had to make certain that his reader did not feel a similar pathos and sympathy for the fallen angels. He reminds us twice in the short passage that the story of Mulciber is only a story: men 'fabled' as they told it, and 'Erring' they relate it.

Pandaemonium is ready, and throngs of angels crowd into the citadel, 'both on the ground and in the air' (767). Milton, like Homer and Virgil before him, faced with a crowd, likens them to bees about their hive who

[27]

Fly to and fro, or on the smoothèd plank,
The suburb of their straw-built citadel,
New rubbed with balm, expatiate and confer
Their state affairs. (I, 772–5)

The simile cuts Pandaemonium down to size and when the great angels are at a stroke literally reduced to 'less than smallest dwarfs' in order to get them in to the assembly, we realise that Milton is playing with them, belittling them for the moment. He compares them to

that pygmean race
Beyond the Indian mount, or faerie elves,
Whose midnight revels, by a forest side
Or fountain some belated peasant sees,
Or dreams he sees, while overhead the moon
Sits arbitress, and nearer to the earth
Wheels her pale course … (I, 780–86)

There is an ominous edge of danger in this simile, but still the transition from hell to the fairies of *A Midsummer Night's Dream* and of folk-lore marks a trivialisation of these foot-soldiers of evil who are at once big and potent to destroy and small as elves in any context of good. Having reduced their 'shapes immense' to 'smallest forms', Milton allows himself a joke and comments that now they were

at large,
Though without number still amidst the hall
Of that infernal court. (I, 790–2)

Satan is holding court and the suggestions of hierarchy and royalty continue. Quite separated from the pygmean throng,

far within
And in their own dimensions like themselves
The great seraphic lords and cherubim
In close recess and secret conclave sat
A thousand demi-gods on golden seats … (I, 792–6)

Satan has rebelled against divine monarchy in heaven and seems intent on building up a monarchy in hell. Such repetition is perhaps one of the consequences of rebellion.

BOOK II

WE CONTINUE TO like, to dislike, to condemn, to admire Satan for much of Book II; we accompany him on his astonishing journey from hell to earth. But first there is a halt in the narrative while Milton presents the rhetoric and the ideas of the debaters in the secret conclave (and secrecy in decision-making was alien to Milton and alien generally to democratic principles).

Satan presides from

> High on a throne of royal state which far
> Outshone the wealth of Ormus and of Ind ... (II, 1–2)

The emphasis is on outward and material gorgeousness. Satan's form when he spoke to his angels in Book I 'had yet not lost / All her original brightness' (I, 592), and there were still traces of the inner spiritual glory of the 'archangel ruin'd'. Here, the brightness comes from gold and a dependence not upon the spirit but upon 'a safe unenvied throne' (23).

There are four speakers in the debate, which is not about the morality of war but about its method only, whether this should be 'open war or covert guile' (41) against 'the thunderer'. Milton gives full play to argument, ideas and rhetoric in these leisured speeches; the characters of the speakers emerge and we have a sense of being in a verse-drama which may well reflect something of the proceedings of the Long Parliament. The first speaker is Moloch, always fierce, Milton tells us, but now 'fiercer by despair'. He is direct: 'My sentence is for open war'. His plain blunt manner pretends humility but declares his pride in himself:

> of wiles,
> More unexpert, I boast not ... (II, 51–2)

He has great contempt for scheming and contriving:

> [wiles] let those
> Contrive who need, or when they need, not now.
> For while they sit contriving, shall the rest,
> Millions that stand in arms, and longing wait
> The signal to ascend, sit lingering here
> Heaven's fugitives, and for their dwelling place
> Accept this dark opprobrious den of shame,
> The prison of his tyranny who reigns
> By our delay? No ... (II, 52–60)

And so the blustering rhetoric goes on, developing the notion that by physical struggle the fallen host will ascend again to heaven; 'The ascent is easy then', asserts Moloch, forgetting Virgil's more realistic pronouncement, as his hero, Aeneas, prepares to go down to the Underworld, that it was descent that was easy, 'facilis descensus Averno' (*Aeneid*, VI, 126); it was ascending that was hard work. And if fighting failed, the rebel angels, in Moloch's view, would either be lucky enough to be annihilated, or, unable to be in more pain than they already were, would continue in nuisance value to 'disturb his heaven', make

> perpetual inroads to alarm,
> Though inaccessible, his fatal throne:
> Which if not victory is yet revenge. (II, 103–5).

'He ended frowning', concludes Milton, and this simple soldier is replaced by Belial, a smooth talker, warns Milton, who can

> make the worse appear
> The better reason ... (II, 113–4)

Belial soon points out that heaven is impregnable and he demolishes Moloch's grounding of 'courage on despair / And utter dissolution' (126–7); consciousness must be retained at any cost,

> for who would lose,
> Though full of pain, this intellectual being,
> Those thoughts that wander through eternity,
> To perish rather, swallowed up and lost
> In the wide womb of uncreated night,
> Devoid of sense and motion? (II, 146–51)

This is another pæan to the freedom of the mind, and an expression of horror at the anonymity of death; we might be reminded of Claudio's great outburst in *Measure for Measure* against the 'cold obstruction' and the rotting of death,

> This sensible warm motion to become
> A kneaded clod and the delighted spirit ...
> To be imprisoned in the viewless winds ... (III, i, 118–25)

In a rush of rhetorical questions Belial then envisages for his listeners a scenario such as Moloch would produce, where the intellectual being would be at the mercy of the enemy's 'red right hand' and would undergo far worse torments than those already suffered; vivid, horrific tortures are listed and Belial concludes in a vague terror of existing

> Unrèspited, unpitied, unreprieved,
> Ages of hopeless end ... (II, 185–6)

and in these lines of infinite and desperate negatives we catch and even intensify the rhythms and sufferings of Hamlet's father's ghost, cut off from God,

> Unhouseled, dis-appointed, unaneled
> > (*Hamlet*, I, v, 77)

So Belial advises that no action be taken for fear of worse suffering, and even holds out the hope that 'Our supreme foe in time may much remit / His anger' (210–11), or 'Not mind us not offending'. Finally and desperately he suggests that they all might get used to the heat and the pain and the darkness. Milton is contemptuous:

[33]

Thus Belial with words clothed in reason's garb
Counselled ignoble ease, and peaceful sloth,
Not peace. (II, 226–8)

Mammon, the third speaker, agrees that war is nonsense and declares that no terms exist that could allow them back into heaven:

Suppose he should relent
And publish grace to all, on promise made
Of new subjection; with what eyes could we
Stand in his presence humble ... (II, 237–40)

How could they sing 'warbled hymns' and 'Forced hallelujahs'?

how wearisome
Eternity so spent in worship paid
To whom we hate. (II, 247–9)

In the world we know, leaders of failed revolutions tend to be executed, but there is a more general application of the dilemma raised by Mammon: it is that of the difficulty people, even Christians, have in accepting forgiveness. Mammon cannot conceive repentance and his alternative is to discount heaven, to seek

Our own good from ourselves, and from our own
Live to ourselves, though in this vast recess,
Free, and to none accountable, preferring
Hard liberty before the easy yoke
Of servile pomp. (II, 253–7)

There seems to be a humanist courage and a grandeur about the preference for 'Hard liberty', but then we realise that liberty means for Mammon the freedom to imitate heaven in hell, the freedom to reproduce heaven's light by the ingenious use of the materials of hell, to

raise
Magnificence; and what can heaven show more? (II, 272–3)

He forgets, of course, in his desire to build a rival 'nether empire' that the light of heaven is more than physical; 'hidden lustre, gems and gold' will not banish hell's spiritual darkness, but the appeal to isolationism, to a kind of national pride is strong, and Milton stresses the welcome given by these weary angels to Mammon's plan, for

> such another field [of battle]
> They dreaded worse than hell. (II, 292–3)

They feel the relief of 'seafaring men o'erwatched' who hear among the rocks the remnants only of all-night blustering winds after a tempest at sea.

The fourth speaker, Beelzebub, rose,

> than whom,
> Satan except, none higher sat ...
> And in his rising seemed
> A pillar of state ... (II, 299–302)

He is a Cromwellian figure,

> princely counsel in his face yet shone,
> Majestic though in ruin: (II, 304–5)

a statesman who knows even how to rise to his feet, and purely by his presence command silence,

> his look
> Drew audience and attention still as night
> Or summer's noontide air ... (II, 307–9)

To address the rebel angels by their former titles is a soothing rhetorical device that Satan had used (and, of course, the avoidance of personal names is a courteous convention of parliamentary debate – Milton's model for this debate in hell). Beelzebub begins:

> Thrones and imperial powers, offspring of heaven
> Ethereal virtues ... (II, 310–11)

[35]

but then he shocks his audience into a recognition of the reality they have chosen; should they not rather be called

> Princes of hell? For so the popular vote
> Inclines, here to continue, and build up here
> A growing empire; (II, 313–5)

Each previous speaker's solution is demolished, the bleakest future is envisaged, and then, out of the desperate situation, as though a sudden thought strikes him, Beelzebub speaks of the new created world and its inhabitants and the need to learn more about their world. Some 'advantageous act' might be achieved, either

> To waste his whole creation, or possess
> All as our own, and drive as we were driven,
> The puny habitants, or if not drive,
> Seduce them to our party, that their God
> May prove their foe … (II, 365–9)

Satan's attention of course had already turned in this direction (I, 651–9) and we realise that, as in so many executive meetings, the chairman and his next-in-command have pre-arranged the substance of the concluding speech in the debate. Beelzebub's plan describes a terrible revenge (and it is one too frequently resorted to by the bullies of this world, to 'drive as we were driven'); the only way for the devils of *Paradise Lost* to think of any comfort is to make others feel the loss that they have felt, repeat the deprivation they have known; there might thus be a vengeance in thwarting the Creator. Milton stresses the conscious need to have a re-enactment of their fall by using, and again at the emphatic beginning of a line, the words used of Satan at his fall, 'Hurled headlong'. Beelzebub conjures up the joy in hell when God's

> darling sons
> Hurled headlong to partake with us, shall curse
> Their frail original, and faded bliss,
> Faded so soon. Advise if this be worth

Attempting, or to sit in darkness here
Hatching vain empires. (II, 373–8)

'faded bliss / Faded so soon': there is triumph, not lament, in Beelzebub's repetition, and when Adam later meets the newly-fallen Eve and

From his slack hand the garland wreathed for Eve
Down dropped, and all the faded roses shed, (IX, 892–3)

we recall with the quickly 'faded roses' the bliss faded so soon, foretold so early in the poem and thereafter a threat. Words in *Paradise Lost* often thus echo themselves and enrich the poem's musical and meaningful texture.

Beelzebub's plan is even joyfully and unanimously approved, and the only question is,

Whom shall we send
In search of this new world, whom shall we find
Sufficient? Who shall tempt with wandering feet
The dark unbottomed infinite abyss
And through the palpable obscure find out
His uncouth way, or spread his airy flight
Upborne with indefatigable wings
Over the vast abrupt ere he arrive
The happy isle? (II, 402–10)

We note the directionless 'wandering feet'. 'Wandering', like 'fading', or 'woe', is one of the poem's repeated words; we have already read of Belial's 'thoughts that wander through eternity' (II, 148); soon a group of rebel angels will discuss philosophy, and find 'no end, in wandering mazes lost' (II, 561); another group, following 'inclination or sad choice', will be led 'per-plexed', 'wandering each his several way' over the physical landscape of hell (II, 523–5), and here, in this passage the ad-venturer who will have to penetrate the hazards of Chaos will 'tempt with wandering feet / The dark unbottomed infinite abyss'. In every case, whether physical or metaphysical, there is a sense involved with 'wandering', that certainty, the key to purposive definition and truth, has been lost. Such insecurity, for fallen angel or fallen man, whether of thought or place, is an aspect of hell. We will find this sense of insecurity and loss of direction at the end of the poem when Adam and Eve, exiled from Paradise,

> ... hand in hand with wandering steps and slow,
> Through Eden took their solitary way. (XII, 648–9)

They are bewildered as they take their first wandering steps into a colder world, but their lot, unlike that of the fallen angels, is mixed; they are not totally lost; although solitary individuals, they are companions, hand in hand; they have no home, but providence, we have just been told, is their guide. For them the wandering is tempered with hope.

Chaos, occupying part of the space between hell and earth in the poem's cosmos, is a huge image of insecurity. In Beelzebub's evocation of it, Milton piles adjective upon adjective (even as an unstable adjective shades off into the function of a noun: 'palpable obscure', 'vast abrupt'); there is nothing firm to step upon, no level ground, and no certain syntax. The voyager, one moment 'upborne', the next hovering above the falls of 'the vast abrupt', must keep 'indefatigable wings'; the word 'indefatigable' is hard to say in a blank verse line and suggests the energy that will be required.

There is silence in hell; no-one offers to make the journey. At last,

> Satan, whom now transcendent glory raised
> Above his fellows, with monarchal pride
> Conscious of highest worth, unmoved thus spake. (II, 427–9)

In pride Satan offers himself, emphasising the terrors he will undergo and his sense of responsibility as leader:

> Wherefore do I assume
> These royalties ... (II, 450–1)

In the next book of *Paradise Lost* there will be not quite a debate but an assessment of the developing situation, and there will be another offering, this time by the Son of God who too will go to earth, his purpose the opposite of Satan's: to save, not destroy. The Son makes his offer in no self-aggrandising spirit, and the reader sees Satan in the light of Christ and *vice versa* because the parallel structures direct us to make comparisons. Such larger parallelisms, like the echoing words, help draw into oneness this massive poem.

But Satan does offer himself and he knows the cost:

> long is the way
> And hard, that out of hell leads up to light ... (II, 432–3)

Hell is darkness; even from flames there was 'no light but rather darkness visible'. Milton in blindness knew this hell as he wrote *Paradise Lost*, and he now presents Satan, wandering, lost and floundering through hell and Chaos, as something of an epic hero striving towards the 'glimmering dawn' that ultimately penetrates the far borders of Chaos. And in yet another sense there is something not unheroic about the solitary journey that Satan undertakes: he rises immediately after his offer,

> prevented all reply,
> Prudent, lest from his resolution raised
> Others among the chief might offer now –
> (Certain to be refused) ... (II, 467–70)

He goes alone on a voyage of discovery, as it were the modern seventeenth-century man, testing on his own person the limits of the known world and pushing against the boundaries of ignorance. But first, and before the 'Stygian council' dissolves, the very angels who had rebelled, who had withheld their service from God, offer worship to Satan,

> Towards him they bend
> With awful reverence prone; and as a god
> Extol him ... (II, 477–9)

They too, as Eve will, as Adam will, forget the Creator in homage to his Creation.

On Satan's departure his followers, like the armies in epic

[39]

poems when there is an interlude of peace, turn to exercises and various pursuits. Their 'rejoicing in their matchless chief' (II, 487) gives them a delight such as comes from an evening of 'radiant sun' after a day when

> the louring element
> Scowls o'er the darkened landscape snow, or shower;

In this simile as the weather changes we move symbolically out of hell and onto the beautiful earth where

> the fields revive,
> The birds their notes renew, and bleating herds
> Attest their joy, that hill and valley rings. (II, 488–95)

It is the universally loved sounds here (and the blind poet was particularly sensitive to sound) that declare the goodness of earth and remind us of earth's innocence as Satan journeys towards it and carries with him the spirit of malevolence.

The peace among the devils as they wait for Satan's return causes Milton to break out of his own poem – as he does more than once – and express open anger at the wasteful conflicts of his own day:

> O shame to men! Devil with devil damned
> Firm concord holds, men only disagree
> Of creatures rational, though under hope
> Of heavenly grace … (II, 496–9)

Some of the fallen angels play noisy aggressive games; others make even more noise as they

> Rend up both rocks and hills, and ride the air
> In whirlwind; hell scarce holds the wild uproar. (II, 540–1)

The pain that such loud confusion would cause Milton is suggested by the pain in the simile used to describe the unbearable noise. Milton famously thinks of Alcides (Hercules) inadvertently putting on and unable to take off the shirt soaked in burning poison; Alcides

> felt the envenomed robe, and tore
> Through pain up by the roots Thessalian pines ... (II, 543–4)

There is no need to mention the roar of agony or the sounds of pines wrenched up like hair from the head; we register these in the violent effort to deflect the pain onto something outside the body, and in the contorted choked word-order of the phrases: the main verb 'tore' at the end of the line, the adverb 'up' not next to its verb, 'tore up', but delayed, 'through pain', and delayed again by a depth of pain, 'up by the roots', and finally the object of the verb 'Thessalian pines'. Except for 'Thessalian' the words are grim monosyllables.

Milton then characteristically moves to the very opposite of this dissonance, for some fallen angels

>   sing
> With notes angelical to many a harp
> Their own heroic deeds and hapless fall
> By doom of battle ... (II, 547–50)

The angels in heaven (in Book III) sing of God's deeds and his Creation, while here the fallen angels sing of their own deeds, extol (as national groups do) their own heroic past and complain – laying dubious claim to the phrase 'free virtue' –

>   that fate
> Free virtue should enthral to force or chance. (II, 551–2)

As Milton remarks,

> Their song was partial, but the harmony
> (What could it less when spirits immortal sing?)
> Suspended hell, and took with ravishment
> The thronging audience. (II, 552–5)

Again, there is art in hell, as well as, in the poem, Milton's art in evoking it, drawing out the harmony, making us wait for the 'harmony ... Suspended', by placing between the noun 'harmony' and the verb 'Suspended' a parenthesis that itself suspends the sentence.

Others of the fallen angels take to that favourite pursuit of intellectuals – talking; endlessly talking philosophy,

> (For eloquence the soul, song charms the sense ... (II, 556)

They reason about

> providence, foreknowledge, will, and fate,
> Fixed fate, free will, foreknowledge absolute ... (II, 559–60)

They argue about good and evil, happiness and final misery, but though their discourse charms the time for the moment, exerts a 'pleasing sorcery', their ideas do not move forward, lacking God-directed energy; they are in stasis, and

> found no end, in wandering mazes lost. (II, 561)

Troops of others, 'adventurous bands', explore the geography of hell, but their eyes 'found / No rest'; they encounter every aspect of landscape that the seventeenth-century imagination recoiled from:

> through many a dark and dreary vale
> They passed, and many a region dolorous,
> O'er many a frozen, many a fiery alp,
> Rocks, caves, lakes, fens, bogs, dens, and shades of death,
> A universe of death, which God by curse
> Created evil, for evil only good ... (II, 618–23)

The mountains, lakes and rocks of today's Cumbria would be unacceptable to the cultivated mind of Milton's day; there is a shuddering horror in the mounting monosyllables of 'Rocks, caves ...' (621), and Milton judges such wildness appropriate to hell; hell is a landscape abandoned by God, even cursed by him; it is meaningless. We realise this when we come to Milton's conception of the nature that is meaningful, the nature of the Garden; this last nature is a book from which we may read divine goodness.

For the rest of Book II we are with Satan in his journey towards earth; we fly close to 'the superior fiend', keeping almost as close to him as Virgil was to Dante in the latter's epic, now shaving 'with level wing the deep', now soaring 'Up to the fiery concave towering high' (635). There are wonderful opportunities in *Paradise Lost* for a film-maker who likes special effects; the early illustrators saw what riches there were, and used them brilliantly in their own way. As Satan reaches the massive outer gates of hell the subject-matter of Milton's poem begins to resemble old-fashioned, almost medieval, allegorical drama where the personages carry a dominant moral or psychological meaning. There are two shapes by the gates:

> one seemed woman to the waist, and fair,
> But ended foul in many a scaly fold ... (II, 650–1)

About the shape's middle and frequently creeping inside and then out of the womb,

> A cry of hell hounds never ceasing barked ... (II, 654)

The other shape seems more formidable as being less defined,

> If shape it might be called that shape had none
> Distinguishable in member, joint or limb,
> Or substance might be called that shadow seemed ...
> (II, 667–9)

The shape, black as night, and wearing 'the likeness of a kingly crown', is hostile to Satan, and Milton sets everything up for a tremendous encounter when the woman/serpent shape

> with hideous outcry rushed between.
> O Father, what intends thy hand, she cried,
> Against thy only son? What fury, O son,
> Possesses thee to bend that mortal dart
> Against thy father's head? (II, 726–30)

There is all the calculated surprise here that will belong to late nineteenth-century melodrama. Satan denies all knowledge:

> I know thee not, nor ever saw till now
> Sight more detestable than him and thee. (II, 744–5)

The portress of hell gate reminds him of her birth:

[43]

>   shining heavenly fair, a goddess armed
>   Out of thy head I sprung: (II, 757–8)

This had happened as Satan traitorously presided over the first
conspiratorial meeting of the rebel angels; they called the 'goddess armed' Sin, and so the allegory becomes clear: Satan has
withdrawn his love from God; alone he brings forth Sin in a
parody of divine generation, and then, as Sin explains, he desires her. She reminds him how much she pleased him then,

>   Thy self in me thy perfect image viewing ... (II, 764)

Satan can have no love outside himself; there is a narcissism
about his incestuous union. In a violent birth that distorts her
body, Sin produces the second horrific and pugnacious shape
at the gate. The hellish trinity has been generated. Death, Sin's
offspring, continues the pattern; he pursues and rapes his
mother again and again. Monstrous little barking deaths are
born who constantly creep back into the womb of Sin to get
nourishment. Sin's body has become in its lower part the foul
serpent Satan now sees, for Sin, in Milton's view, may have a
fair face but is profoundly foul and gives birth to little deaths
that retain a persistent existence.

As Milton creates this allegory we see that in Satan's case
Sin and Death result from the withdrawal of his love from God;
he is sole author of the hell he makes and must endure. There
will be mitigating circumstances for Eve and for Adam; their
Fall is a response to temptation from outside themselves. Or is
it entirely? And how much does God, who knows and foresees
all, not only permit but will the Falls, both of them? Such
questions will continue to arise. But here, in Book II, Milton
has changed his narrative approach for this allegorical story;
he goes back to something out of Satan's past, to aspects of his
psychological make-up that became part of him before we first
meet him, before we find him in so many ways to have the
makings of a hero. Is it that Milton must be certain at this point
in the story, before he allows Satan to set foot on earth, that
the reader will be convinced that Satan is indeed an evil spirit

and the author of evil? Milton will need the reader to direct sympathy not to Satan but to the human pair. Can we entirely endorse Dr Johnson's view:

> This unskilful allegory appears to me one of the greatest faults of the poem.

Or can we defend the allegory by suggesting that it functions in an alternative way, and a way that has a universal reach, of indicating the single-mindedness of revenge: to repeat upon others the original self-inflicted injuries through love turned inward, through pride in the self, through the repetition of sin and the constant spawning of death, small deaths where aspects of the self die again and again. Satan wants others to know the Death-in-Life that he knows. Such allegorical projections, before Freud, before psychoanalysis, are projections of how the mind can work.

After this allegorical excursion to the further past, Milton returns us to the narrative, and Satan, now excessively polite, explains his 'wandering quest' to his 'Dear Daughter' and assures 'my fair son here' that he will be 'fed and filled / Immeasurably, all things shall be your prey' (843–4). Sin and Death are very pleased at the thought of dwelling at ease upon the earth and going 'up and down unseen'. The gates are opened and cannot be closed. Satan

> Stood on the brink of hell and looked a while … (II, 918)

We too look at Chaos, primal matter as when 'the earth was without form, and void; and darkness was upon the face of the deep' (Genesis, 1: 2). As readers we have been moving in tense from Satan's earlier past to the narrative past to the future of universal death, and now, with Chaos, to a past that belongs to a time before time. Movements of tense are a feature of *Paradise Lost*, and they contribute to the reader's sense of instability; fallen, we are insecure, and the poem reflects this. Chance rules Chaos, and Satan is subject to it; he has little control over his flight through it. He drops into a 'vast vacuity' where his wings can make no impact; he is hurried, 'as many miles aloft'.

He is the sport of chance; his physical strength can scarcely compete. Milton's angels are corporeal; they are not, as was usually thought, simply bodiless spirits. Milton gives Satan a hard time:

> eagerly the fiend
> O'er bog or steep, through straight, rough, dense, or rare,
> With head, hands, wings or feet pursues his way,
> And swims or sinks, or wades, or creeps, or flies ...
>
> (II, 947–50)

The crowding heavily-stressed syllables do not make for a smooth blank verse line; even in saying the words we imitate in little Satan's effort and notice that the erstwhile great archangel in his need to begin revenge is willing to accept humiliation, to creep, to use any means to make his wandering way through Chaos,

> The womb of nature and perhaps her grave ... (II, 911)

This line, a warning to the seventeenth century, is even more ominous now when there are real fears that we might destroy nature and return to Chaos. Satan gets through the confusion and the noise: the noise is far worse than those sounds of recent Civil War, 'battering engines bent to raze / Some capital city (923–4). Milton knew that noise; cities such as Oxford had been under siege, and gave Milton imagery which he relegates to Chaos. But Satan, like Ulysses, with whom he is compared, has the epic hero's endurance and

> now at last the sacred influence
> Of light appears, and from the walls of heaven
> Shoots far into the bosom of dim Night
> A glimmering dawn. (II, 1034–7)

He pauses, and sees 'Far off the empyreal heaven', its

> opal towers and battlements adorned
> Of living sapphire, once his native seat;
> And fast by hanging in a golden chain

This pendent world, in bigness as a star
Of smallest magnitude close by the moon. (II, 1049–53)

That we first see earth's universe, our universe, through Satan's eyes is itself a threat. Though beautifully balanced in the cosmos, and fastened by a chain to heaven, our whole known universe seems remote, tiny and frail. Book II ends with Satan rushing towards it.

BOOK III

THE 'SACRED INFLUENCE / Of light' that is seen as 'a glimmering dawn' towards the end of Book II has become with the first
words of Book III the only light, the light of Godhead. Milton
and the reader have been long in darkness and in hell, and before going with Satan on the last stages of his journey to earth,
we move to hell's opposite, heaven. We begin with Light itself:

> Hail, holy Light, offspring of heaven, first-born ... (III, 1)

Certainly the first thing God created was Light, 'Let there be
light', he says in Genesis; but the theological scholar in Milton
cannot leave it there: God not only created light, he actually,
says St John, is Light, and so Light is perhaps co-eternal with
God:

> Or of the eternal co-eternal beam ... (III, 2)

The Son also is Light; is he offspring or co-eternal or somehow
both? Is he indivisible with God? Hardly surprisingly, Milton
feels that his boldness, perhaps in putting God into a poem at
all, might be reprehensible,

> May I express thee unblamed? Since God is light
> And never but in unapproachèd light
> Dwelt from eternity, dwelt then in thee,
> Bright effluence of bright essence increate. (III, 3–6)

The concentration upon abstraction in these first six lines leads
us to no immediate account of the relationship of God to Light
or of God to the Son; But the patterning speaks: there are the
words 'light' (used three times) and rhyming with 'bright' (used
twice), 'eternal' near to 'co-eternal' and 'eternity', 'dwelt' (used
twice); there is the balance of the last line where 'effluence' and

[49]

'essence' – issue and central source – seem at once separate and inseparable, because both are bright, because they are similar in sound, and because neither has been created. Milton can control words in so many ways; his music here is different from that of his narrative blank verse lines or concrete descriptions. Here, the words retain a sense of mystery, and they dazzle with light. The indivisibility of holiness and light continues with a further polite query as to how Holy Light / God / the Son of God might prefer ('hear'st thou rather') to be addressed:

> Or hear'st thou rather pure ethereal stream,
> Whose fountain who shall tell? (III, 7–8)

From what spring or fountain does such a stream flow, a stream that is ethereal – more airy than any atmosphere – and touched with the spiritual? We are moving towards physical light on earth and Milton's appreciation of this is intense; he speaks in his own person, continuing to address Light:

> Thee I revisit now with bolder wing,
> Escaped the Stygian pool ...
> With other notes than to the Orphean lyre
> I sung of Chaos and eternal Night,
> Taught by the heavenly Muse to venture down
> The dark descent, and up to reascend
> Though hard and rare: thee I revisit safe ... (III, 13–21)

The poet too had been in hell alongside Satan; and in that obscure darkness had sung no sweet song such as Orpheus in the underworld sang when he almost 'won the ear / Of Pluto, to have quite set free / His half-regained Eurydice' ('L'Allegro', 148–50). After his poetic darkness and deprivation Milton addresses Light like a lover, 'Thee I revisit now ... thee I revisit safe'; his relief is evident, but, and for the first time in the poem, Milton discusses his own blindness as again he addresses Light:

> but thou
> Revisit'st not these eyes, that roll in vain
> To find thy piercing ray, and find no dawn; (III, 22–4)

We feel the physical torment in 'eyes that roll in vain', and remember that in Milton's view suffering such as his is a consequence of the Fall; it is a fraction of 'all our woe'. Milton is himself fallen man; he knows man's loss and darkness,

> Yet not the more
> Cease I to wander where the Muses haunt
> Clear spring, or shady grove, or sunny hill … (III, 26–8)

The Muses for Milton haunt chiefly the brooks of Sion where the poet 'nightly' visits for sacred song; he also keeps close to the great blind prophets and poets of the past, including Homer. With such preparation he can

> feed on thoughts, that voluntary move
> Harmonious numbers; as the wakeful bird
> Sings darkling, and in shadiest covert hid
> Tunes her nocturnal note. (III, 37–40)

The wakeful bird, the nightingale, we are thus reminded, sings her beautiful song out of darkness; and darkness for Philomel (who became the nightingale in Ovid's tale) was, like Milton's darkness, the darkness of suffering as well as of night. Creativity for fallen man, the 'harmonious numbers' of Milton's poem, his song, comes out of pain, and Milton here almost cries out in pain at his own relentless darkness:

> Thus with the year
> Seasons return, but not to me returns
> Day, or the sweet approach of even or morn,
> Or sight of vernal bloom, or summer's rose,
> Or flocks, or herds, or human face divine;
> But cloud in stead, and ever-during dark
> Surrounds me, from the cheerful ways of men
> Cut off, and for the book of knowledge fair
> Presented with a universal blank
> Of nature's works to me expunged and razed,
> And wisdom at one entrance quite shut out. (III, 40–50)

The great comfort of being witness to the returning seasons

and years and days is denied to Milton. God had not, even after the Fall, denied this to fallen man:

> While the earth remaineth, seed-time and harvest, and
> cold and heat, and summer and winter, and day and
> night shall not cease. (Gen. 8: 22)

In Eden there is perpetual spring but Milton, in his condition of life mortal and blind, considers the fallen world in all its changes from day to night, from spring flower to summer's rose, from agriculture to man with his paradoxical 'human face divine'; Milton considers all this that he cannot see and finds the fallen world entirely beautiful, the ways of men cheerful and with something of divinity about them. But for him, shut in upon himself, the book of nature is a book destroyed. Milton is at a low point; the Christian epic he is writing is his own personal journey as well as universal myth. He is not the high flier here of Book I that 'with no middle flight intends to soar'; he is a suppliant. Might it be that his own over-weening ambition has caused him, like Satan, to fall into darkness? He concludes his invocation to Book III by returning to address Light,

> So much the rather thou celestial Light
> Shine inward ... (III, 51–2)

Accepting now his physical darkness, he does not ask to be returned to the 'cheerful ways of men', nor refers with the word 'celestial' to the physical light of heaven which Satan had so mourned when he first arrived in hell and had to receive in exchange

> this mournful gloom
> For that celestial light? (I, 244–5)

The celestial light for Milton now will be an inner light:

> the mind through all her powers
> Irradiate, there plant eyes, all mist from thence
> Purge and disperse, that I may see and tell
> Of things invisible to mortal sight. (III, 52–5)

With the same imagery of weather and of planting Milton ends triumphantly, and in a mood of creative strength: 'there plant eyes'; the image is extreme, for the need is great; the tone is urgent, yet the rhythm is secure and confident in the faith that celestial light will irradiate the mind. We have been given in little, through the rehearsal of the personal story of Milton's blindness, the shape of *Paradise Lost* as a whole: that out of loss and suffering, if faith is there, can come a peace and a new and a creative human energy.

Celestial light has much to do, for God is famously invisible to mortal sight, and God now has to come into the poem. Milton avoids description. God's power is implicit in that Milton gives us God's own view of his creation. 'High throned above all highth' God 'bent down his eye' (III, 58). Beyond the angelic host 'thick as stars' about him, and beyond that 'radiant image of his glory', his only Son, he saw 'in the happy garden' of earth 'our two first parents',

> Reaping immortal fruits of joy and love,
> Uninterrupted joy, unrivalled love
> In blissful solitude. (III, 67–9)

We watch, *voyeurs* with God, knowing that a fruit of mortal taste will soon change the happy garden and its blissful lovers. God's eye then moves to 'Hell and the gulf between, and Satan there'. He sees Satan land 'on the bare outside of this world' (74), ready to enter our universe, and turns to speak to his Son, going over what is to happen: that man will 'transgress', will hearken to Satan's 'glozing lies', will fall:

> whose fault?
> Whose but his own? Ingrate, he had of me
> All he could have; I made him just and right,
> Sufficient to have stood, though free to fall. (III, 96–9)

The logic of God's position is mirrored in these short sharp lines, with the alliteration in the last one giving emphasis to God's assertion that man had free choice. So had the angels:

Such I created all th'ethereal powers
And spirits, both them who stood and them who failed;
Freely they stood who stood, and fell who fell. (III, 100–2)

The same firm oppositions of language describe here the same situation, the same freedom, the same strength in standing.

They also serve who only stand and wait,

Milton had concluded in his Sonnet upon his Blindness, contrasting his own enforced inactivity with those who 'post o'er land and ocean without rest'. Some part of Milton is always suspicious of desperate activity, whether in actions or in language. Satan's busyness in bringing order to his followers, his feverish movements through Hell and Chaos, swimming, sinking, wading, creeping, his rhetoric with its dramatic changes of register, all this is contrasted with God who simply sits in heaven, looks down and speaks calmly. Some readers find God's logical calm quite baffling, and more so, his unswerving position that his own foreknowledge did not determine the angels' fall, and will not determine man's. He is not, he declares, responsible. It is a difficult point in Christian doctrine, and Milton was not alone in believing that God's total and timeless knowledge can co-exist with man's mature and responsible freedom of choice. At the end of his first speech God notes that the angels fell 'self-tempted, self-depraved' (130); he does not go into the thorny question of how such a situation of depravity might arise in heaven since he, God, was responsible for the angels' creation. He then concedes in his fair and just way that man, unlike the angels, will be tempted from outside, 'man falls deceived / By the other first: man therefore shall find grace' (130–1). It is dispassionately spoken and the final note is therefore that 'mercy first and last shall brightest shine' (134).

It is not hard to see why readers have tended to find God unattractive. He can have no inner life, no secret thoughts, no pain, no excitement, no fear, no anxiety, no change or growth. He is what he appears to be. And so he comes across as a flat character; Satan, on the other hand, has lived with an inner world and a changing world since he entered the poem. Nor can the Son have an inner life, but he does have a more active function than the Father: he had been the champion against the rebel angels in the final phase of the War in Heaven (to be described in Book VI). Here, in Book III, we see him in Heaven talking with his father and of course replicating his father,

> in him all his Father shone
> Substantially expressed, and in his face
> Divine compassion visibly appeared,
> Love without end, and without measure grace. (III, 139–42)

The eternal face of divine goodness can only be one face but it is love rather than justice that shines from the Son's face. He speaks his hope that when man shall have fallen he shall not 'finally be lost ... / Thy creature late so loved, thy youngest son' (150–1). He almost woos the Father not to destroy:

> That be from thee far,
> That far be from thee, Father ... (III, 153–4)

The soft 'f's and the repeated vowels here, the almost repeated phrases placed together, would take Milton's bible-reading readers back to Genesis (18: 25) where Abraham pleaded – in vain – with God not to destroy totally Sodom and Gomorrah: 'That be far from thee to do after this manner, to slay the righteous with the wicked.' Out of this Milton makes an exquisite pattern of rhythm, alliteration and vowel sounds, and, of course, as God knew all along,

> Man shall not quite be lost, but saved who will,
> Yet not of will in him, but grace in me
> Freely vouchsafed; (III, 173–5)

God speaks about grace, about prayer and about the hope of repentance, and then indicates that the cost of such powerful grace must be a voluntary death, a sacrifice made for man's sake. He invites the angels to offer,

> but all the heavenly choir stood mute,
> And silence was in heaven ... (III, 217–8)

[55]

The situation parallels the consultation in hell; there, Satan had made the offer to go to earth in pursuit of revenge; here, the Son makes the corresponding offer to go to earth to save mankind, and undergo an earthly death. There is nothing to debate; God is pleased, and declares that the Son is now Son of Man as well as Son of God, and worthy by merit as well as birthright to be universal king. 'All knees to thee shall bow'. Ultimately the Son will preside over Judgment Day, and after that there will be

> New heaven and earth, wherein the just shall dwell ...
>
> (III, 335)

The Son then will need

> no regal sceptre ...
> God shall be all in all. (III, 340–5)

There will be no more division, no need of sovereignty. This would be the perfect republic – how distant, how unachievable on earth, even in a compromise form, Milton must sadly have concluded after the Restoration.

The multitude of angels shout their joy, cast down, as is their wont, their golden crowns in a heaven where the pavement shines like a sea of jasper, Elysian flowers grow by the amber waters of heaven's river, and there is no need for Milton to include more than a very few details from the Book of Revelation for us to picture that resplendent New Jerusalem. He had had to be original for the terrain of hell and the architecture of Pandæmonium, for there is no biblical model, but here Milton could rely upon familiarity with the Bible's baroque splendours of the City of God. They 'sung a new song', St John tells us, and in Milton's heaven the angels,

> crowned again, their golden harps they took,
> Harps ever tuned ... (III, 365–6)

and they sing. Milton, a musician himself, carried his horror of discord even to the detail of making the tuning of heavenly instruments unnecessary. The angels sing, all of them. They have

and need only one song, a song in praise of God and the Son;
hell, we recall, because its new dwellers have new experience,
has diverse music. As God cannot be approached directly, the
angels approach his praise largely by way of negatives,

> omnipotent,
> Immutable, immortal, infinite,
> Eternal … (III, 372–4)

The sonorous succession of Latinate adjectives marking God's
non-humanity continues into his being inaccessible, except
remotely and by means of brilliant opposition. There are times,
the angels sing,

> when thou shadest
> The full blaze of thy beams, and through a cloud
> Drawn round about thee like a radiant shrine,
> Dark with excessive bright thy skirts appear,
> Yet dazzle heaven, that brightest seraphim
> Approach not, but with both wings veil their eyes.
>
> (III, 377–82)

'Dark with excessive bright': the adjectival paradox enacts the
unknowable mystery of God, as well as pointing to a known
fact – that we experience a darkness when we look directly
into a bright sun. The angels go on to praise the Son of God,
and Milton himself excitedly joins in, a seventeenth-century
poet entering his poem, singing with his own angelic choir,
and promising the Son,

> thy name
> Shall be the copious matter of my song
> Henceforth … (III, 412–4)

Mammon had referred contemptuously to the 'warbled hymns'
and 'Forced alleluias' (II, 242–3) of the heavenly singing; Milton
joins it, and perhaps hopes his readers in imagination will also
join, thus demonstrating that such acts of praise are tedious
only to those who cannot give themselves spontaneously.

We leave the angels singing and in the second half of Book

III follow Satan in his progress towards earth. Immediately there is action. Upon 'the firm opaceous globe / Of this round world' (418–9), the outer shell of our entire universe,

> Satan alighted walks. (III, 422)

The Chaos that Satan has traversed surrounds this shell that protects the primum mobile, the first moving sphere and the furthest from earth in the old Ptolemaic cosmology. At times, if the fiction of his poem needs it, Milton puts forward a modern Copernican model of the cosmos and he can add details of his own. The size of this poem, the magnificence of its immortal characters, the significance of its action, all these demand, as it were, a science-fiction space element in the physical geography of the poem. Upon 'the firm opaceous globe', Milton repeats,

> Here walked the fiend at large in spacious field.
> As when a vulture … (III, 430–1)

And thus the epic simile comes back into the poem; the rich digressions of simile could have no place in the presentation of heaven, a region absolute and incomparable with inhabitants of perfect integrity. Milton's vulture flies far to find his prey:

> To gorge the flesh of lambs or yeanling kids
> On hills where flocks are fed … (III, 434–5)

the carrion-seeking bird flies from the Arctic to the Ganges, passing through 'the barren plains/Of Sericana' (North West China)

> where Chineses drive
> With sails and wind their cany wagons light:
> So on this windy sea of land, the fiend
> Walked up and down alone bent on his prey … (III, 438–41)

The simile was almost forgetting the vulture in contemplation of the charming landships of China, but sails and wind take Milton back to the 'windy sea of land' where the fiend walks 'bent on his prey'.

We have to wait in some suspense – even though we know the story – for Satan's encounter with 'his prey'. The dramatic meeting with Eve and with Adam cannot come until we have got to know the human characters in their unfallen life in Eden. Meanwhile we remain with Satan as he moves from the outer edge of our universe closer to its centre and finally into Paradise. 'Long he wandered' (499) on the empty and windy sea of land, and Milton seizes the chance to describe what that place will become at a later time: it will be Limbo, and he gives examples of those who will find themselves there – vain builders of Babels, suicides, friars, pilgrims, monks. Limbo is a Paradise of Fools and Milton in this passage is a Protestant satirist. Long, Satan wandered in the empty place, finding finally a dawning light and coming to a set of magnificent steps leading up to the wall of Heaven:

> The stairs were such as whereon Jacob saw
> Angels ascending and descending, bands
> Of guardians bright, when he from Esau fled
> To Padan-Aram in the field of Luz,
> Dreaming by night under the open sky,
> And waking cried, This is the gate of heaven. (III, 510–15)

Jacob was to wrong his brother Esau, but after the wrongs and after his dream of a ladder reaching up to heaven, he would dedicate himself to doing God's work, with ultimately a reconciliation with his brother; Milton may have wanted, fleetingly and ironically, to suggest by his comparison of the stairs with Jacob's ladder that there was still a chance for Satan to repent. Alternatively, the stairs (which were retractable) may have served to

> aggravate
> His sad exclusion from the doors of bliss. (III, 524–5)

Satan stands however on the lowest step, looks down, not up,

> Looks down with wonder at the sudden view
> Of all this world at once. (III, 542–3)

Milton likens Satan's emotion at the panoramic view of our whole universe to that of a scout, a military scout, looking presumably for conquest and possession, who, after a night of peril,

> at last by break of cheerful dawn
> Obtains the brow of some high-climbing hill (III, 545–6)

and sees

> The goodly prospect of some foreign land
> First seen, or some renowned metropolis
> With glistering spires and pinnacles adorned,
> Which now the rising sun gilds with his beams.
> Such wonder seized ... (III, 548–52)

Satan's wonder is emphasised, as a comparable wonder will be for stout Cortez a century and a half later as he stared at the Pacific, 'silent upon a peak in Darien'. The 'goodly states and kingdoms' of Keats's sonnet, 'On First Looking into Chapman's Homer', and the sense of wonder bring to mind Milton's passage here, especially as in both passages ideas of conquest are not far behind. Satan's wonder gives way to 'much more envy ... / At sight of all this world beheld so fair' (553–4). Without a moment's hesitation he plunges into our universe,

> throws
> His flight precipitant and winds with ease
> Through the pure marble air his oblique way
> Amongst innumerable stars ... (III, 562–5)

The stars themselves dance, stars that may be 'happy isles' with people dwelling there; Milton leaves open the possibility of life on other planets. But Satan 'stayed not to enquire'; he moves towards the sun:

> There lands the fiend ... (III, 588)

Satan had been, after all, the archangel of light, and he gravitates towards what had been his natural element.

Milton describes the composition of the sun; it is of gold

and silver, chrysolite and many precious stones, one of which (presumably the philosopher's stone), Milton notes, has always eluded earth's philosophers. This stone

> Philosophers in vain so long have sought,
> In vain, though by their powerful art they bind
> Volatile Hermes, and call up unbound
> In various shapes old Proteus from the sea ... (III, 601–4)

'Old Proteus' had a way of changing shape to evade capture, a way that Satan himself has; evil has a facility in shape-changing, in deception, in, the Puritan might add, in acting, and it is as a 'stripling cherub' that Satan enquires his way of the angel of the sun. Alchemical art might 'call up unbound / In various shapes old Proteus from the sea'; the imagination in a later age might call up this vision of Proteus, and to Wordsworth a hundred and fifty years later such a vision seemed more desirable than any capitulation to his own age of gross materialism, 'Getting and spending', in a world that is 'too much with us',

> Great God! I'd rather be
> A Pagan suckled in a creed outworn;
> So might I, standing on this pleasant lea,
> Have glimpses that would make me less forlorn;
> Have sight of Proteus rising from the sea;
> Or hear old Triton blow his wreathèd horn.
> ('The World is too much with us', 9–14)

Proteus, amorphous matter, the unbound materialism of a pagan world, is yet a wondrous emanation absent from Wordsworth's time. But it is the beauty of Milton's line about him that Wordsworth echoes, and that reminds us that Milton is so often a sensuous writer, and provides the germ of sensuousness for other writers, not least for the Romantics.

Satan, now externally a young stripling cherub eager for knowledge, is the perfect actor, and the archangel Uriel accepts the young cherub's reason for wanting directions for earth – to find out more about 'this new happy race of men' that

> The universal maker we may praise. (III, 676)

Uriel cannot pierce through hypocrisy,

> the only evil that walks
> Invisible, except to God alone ... (III, 683–4)

We might remember this, with understanding, when we come to Eve's fatal succumbing to Satan disguised as a speaking serpent. But for Uriel here, as for Christians from St Augustine to Milton, the true end of knowledge is not knowledge for its own sake but for God's sake, for praise of him arising from a more intense and detailed appreciation of his work. Satisfied with the cherub's motive, Uriel gave Satan directions, and the latter, bowing low, took his leave and, jubilant, threw 'his steep flight in many an airy wheel' (741) and landed upon earth.

BOOK IV

CLOSE INDEED IS Satan now to his prey, but Milton still delays the encounter, and the reader, though perfectly well knowing the outcome, experiences a growing tension and expectancy. Milton himself feels an urgent anxiety about 'our first parents' and longs to warn them. He rushes from his Genesis story to the far off end of the Bible and the far off end of time and wants the voice that St John of Revelation hears cry at the final Apocalypse, 'Woe to the inhabitants on earth!' Milton always wanted to warn: as late as 1659 he wrote *The Ready and Easy Way to Establish a Free Commonwealth and the Excellence thereof compared with the Inconveniences and Dangers of Re-admitting Kingship in this Nation*, published 1660. It was of course far too late to change things, but the pamphlet was for Milton a confession of faith, 'the last words of our expiring liberty', he wrote, and he had felt compelled to speak them, 'though I was sure I should have spoken only to trees and stones and had none to cry to …'. Here, at the beginning of Book IV, with the same fervour, the same impotent fervour, he allows himself the drama of longing to warn Adam and Eve, to stop the inevitable catastrophe of history.

Satan is alone, about to achieve his object, 'Yet not rejoicing' (13), for

> horror and doubt distract
> His troubled thoughts and from the bottom stir
> The hell within him, for within him hell
> He brings … (IV, 18–21)

The inescapable hell is caught in the reflecting circularity of this language:'The hell within him, for within him hell'.There is nowhere else and nothing else; Eden 'in his view / Lay pleasant' and there, from time to time ' his grieved look he fixes sad'

[63]

(27–8), but he is, like Mephistophilis in Marlowe's Elizabethan play *Dr Faustus*, in a condition of permanent exile:

> Why, this is hell, nor am I out of it
> (*The Tragical History of Doctor Faustus*, I, iii, 76)

> ... But where we are is hell,
> And where hell is there must we ever be ...
> (ibid., I, v, 125–6)

explains the devil to Faustus. Hell is a state of mind and Satan explores it, even as Mephistophilis and Faustus, and indeed Shakespeare's Richard III and Macbeth had explored it, in a dramatic form. Milton gives Satan a soliloquy in which Satan mounts a passionate attack upon himself and another upon the Almighty (Satan cannot use the word 'God'); an impassioned analysis of himself with an understanding of his own inevitable ambition even had he been 'some inferior angel'; a longing to repent, with immediately a recoil from such a move; and the social need for his subordinates' admiration. He cannot submit:

> Disdain forbids me and my dread of shame
> Among the spirits beneath whom I seduced ... (IV, 82–3)

He has a realistic sense that were he to

>   obtain
> By act of grace my former state; how soon
> Would height recall high thoughts, how soon unsay
> What feigned submission swore ... (IV, 93–6)

He can imagine repenting his repentance, and so he concludes by reaffirming his identity as negation:

> So farewell hope, and with hope farewell fear,
> Farewell remorse: all good to me is lost;
> Evil be thou my good ... (IV, 108–10)

'Farewell the tranquil mind, farewell content' had been Othello's words as he was led by Iago into his own appalling hell, and we see how Shakespeare's tragic heroes in their agony of mind found in some sort a descendant in Satan. It is worth recalling too that Milton's first published poem was his anonymous tribute to Shakespeare printed in the second Folio edition of Shakespeare's Works, 1632. Milton had been scarcely twenty-one when he wrote in homage to 'my Shakespear ... Dear son of memory, great heir of Fame'. Satan's is a fierce and absolute acceptance of despair. His speech has moved dramatically from its beginning which was an address to the sun:

> O thou that with surpassing glory crowned,
> Look'st from thy sole dominion like the God
> Of this new world ... (IV, 32–4)

The sun's glory is unbearable to Satan, once the Angel of Light,

> how I hate thy beams
> That bring to my remembrance from what state
> I fell, how glorious once above thy sphere ... (IV, 37–9)

Rehearsing his own recent history, Satan forgets that he is addressing the sun; he himself is soon the 'thou' whom he addresses:

> Nay cursed be thou; since against his thy will
> Chose freely what it now so justly rues.
> Me miserable! Which way shall I fly
> Infinite wrath, and infinite despair?
> Which way I fly is hell; myself am hell ... (IV, 71–5)

From the first open address to the sun the speech moves to the 'lowest deep' and from that to an even 'lower deep / Still threatening to devour me' (76–7).

Within the rhythms of speech and complex turns of feeling we reach this despair and recall that when John Aubrey put together some notes on Milton's Life he included information given him by Edward Phillips, Milton's nephew, who remembered verses of 'Satan's exclamation to the sun' from

15 or 16 years before ever his poem was thought of.
Which verses were intended for the beginning of a
tragedy which he had designed; but was diverted from it
by other business.

The revelation, made in the first person, of the chaos in Satan's
mind is indeed the stuff of dramatic tragedy, and Milton,
we know from an early manuscript, had given considerable
thought to the idea of a play on the subject of Paradise Lost.
Satan's earlier rhetorical boast to Beelzebub that 'the mind is
its own place' (I, 254) seems a doom now in the solitude of
exclusion, not a grandeur. Shelley saw 'the sublimest pathos'
in the account here of Satan's inward torture; Hazlitt, putting
Satan at the centre, thought *Paradise Lost* 'the most heroic subject that was ever chosen for a poem'. Humanists generally of
the Romantic period saw Satan as the poem's tragic hero and
the speech at the beginning of Book IV did much to reinforce
this view.

We cannot forget Satan's pain but Milton ensures that we
are jolted out of any dangerous sympathy for him the moment
his soliloquy ends, for the narrative voice lists the passions that
have 'dimmed' the stripling cherub's face and 'betrayed /Him
counterfeit, if any eye beheld' (116–17). The eye that beholds
now is the reader's and, from a distance, as it were from the
point of view of God, the reader sees the inauthentic cherub,
the 'Artificer of fraud' as he smooths 'with outward calm' 'each
perturbation … the first / That practised falsehood under
saintly show' (120–2). Uriel from the sun has also noted Satan's
'gestures fierce'.

With Satan we approach Paradise and Milton describes the
'steep wilderness' of trees, the ranks that 'ascend / Shade above
shade, a woody theatre' (140–41), and from this natural, but
clearly designed citadel,

> The verdurous wall of Paradise upsprung … (IV, 143)

Inside the wall are more trees,

> goodliest trees loaden with fairest fruit,
> Blossoms and fruits at once of golden hue ... (IV, 147–8)

Blossoms and fruits together are a mark of all the timeless gardens of the imagination, and Satan, the reader with him, climbs upward to this protected garden which is within the last and topmost circle of trees. He is contemptuous of the one gate and

> At one slight bound high over leaped all bound ...
>
> (IV, 181)

Milton's witty line offers a perfect emblem of transgression, the violating of boundaries, moral as well as physical. Two similes immediately register stages in Satan's inevitable degradation from the great archangel ruined to the demon of popular story. He is likened to the 'prowling wolf'

> Watching where shepherds pen their flocks at eve
> In hurdled cotes amid the field secure,
> [who] Leaps o'er the fence with ease into the fold:
> Or as a thief bent to unhoard the cash
> Of some rich burgher ...
> In at the window climbs, or o'er the tiles; (IV, 185–91)

The rich burgher in his illusory security behind 'substantial doors / Cross-barred and bolted fast' (189–90) brings into the poem the contemporary fallen fearful city, displacing for a moment the paradisal garden; and the prowling wolf similarly reminds us that the country too in future times will not remain free of predatory greed. Satan, like wolf and thief, is watching and waiting; watching is the first strategy in his attack. He flies, 'for prospect', to the top of the highest tree; ironically, this is the tree of life, appropriated here, as virtue often will be, to the service of evil, and used as a perch by Satan who 'sat like a cormorant' (196) and cast his rapacious eye over Paradise.

That we see Paradise for the first time with Satan as observer is in itself ominous. We see 'All trees of noblest kind for sight, smell, taste' (217); we see the tree of knowledge next to that of life; we see how Milton (following Genesis) contrives, by placing rivers, streams and springs above and underground, to keep all Eden fertile without need of rain; we see the beauty of the place through Milton's presentation of it as jewelled art:

> tell how, if art could tell,
> How from that sapphire fount the crisped brooks,
> Rolling on orient pearl and sands of gold,
> With mazy error under pendant shades
> Ran nectar, visiting each plant, and fed
> Flowers worthy of Paradise which not nice art
> In beds and curious knots, but nature boon
> Poured forth profuse on hill and dale and plain ...
>
> (IV, 236–243)

The Book of Revelation tells us that the eternal landscape of the New Jerusalem will be of gold and precious stones, and here through the same bejewelled metaphor a similar suggestion of permanence hovers over this garden, rendering harmless, or seemingly harmless, the embedded phrase 'mazy error'; but not for long: such words as 'mazy error' will soon carry forebodings of loss. The geometric patterned flower-beds and knot-gardens of Jacobean England form no part of Milton's conception of the ideal garden. His Paradise has a freedom and naturalness that anticipates the eighteenth-century park of Capability Brown. In Milton's 'happy rural seat of various view' (247) are groves of rich trees,

> Betwixt them lawns, or level downs, and flocks
> Grazing the tender herb, were interposed,
> Or palmy hillock, or the flowery lap
> Of some irriguous valley spread her store,
> Flowers of all hue, and without thorn the rose ...
>
> (IV, 252–6)

As landscape gardeners know, the judicious placing of flocks of sheep gives proper animation to the scene; there is a lake, and 'murmuring waters [which] fall / Down the slope hills' (260–1) and become part of nature's harmony:

> The birds their choir apply; airs, vernal airs,
> Breathing the smell of field and grove, attune
> The trembling leaves … (IV, 264–6)

The breezes of the eternal spring bring spring's fragrances from the fields and groves, and at the same time they seem themselves to be not just air, but airs, tunes, melodies, that make music, 'attune / The trembling leaves' of trees to the choir of birds and the murmuring of waters. The garden is pure sensuous delight. Milton's description of Eden undoubtedly influenced the design of many country house pleasure grounds; it probably encouraged too the planting of trees, 'trees of noblest kind', from all over the world – the making of arboreta. Attempts to re-create Paradise, at least in terms of place, abound.

Milton evokes four other celebrated gardens but none can compare with the original Paradise,

> Not that fair field
> Of Enna, where Proserpine gathering flowers
> Herself a fairer flower by gloomy Dis
> Was gathered, which cost Ceres all that pain
> To seek her through the world … (IV, 268–72)

There is danger for the beautiful girl in the beautiful place, as soon there will be for Eve, alone like Proserpine among her flowers, 'Herself … fairest unsupported flower' (IX, 432), and to be gathered not physically as Proserpine by the king of the Underworld, but mentally by Satan, king of the mind's as well as the external underworld. There is a massive cost in each case to redeem the girl from death: it 'cost Ceres all that pain' but the parallel makes us recognise differences: Eve will collude in her Fall, and it will cost her (and all humanity, and God himself) a never-ending experience and consciousness of suffering. These two images of vulnerability, each a girl in a garden, catch up with one another across the vast spaces of *Paradise Lost*, and they help, along with repeated words and phrases, to draw the poem into one-ness and emphasise the inescapable menace that hangs over humanity: Satan is there in Book IV, unbeknown to

Adam and Eve, watching and preparing; he is there in Book IX watching Eve again and ready now to pounce; he is there in the form of 'gloomy Dis', masculine aggression, carrying off a defenceless victim; the paradise which is innocence is always and constantly under siege.

What Satan and the reader see after viewing the garden are, finally, Adam and Eve,

> erect and tall,
> Godlike erect, with native honour clad
> In naked majesty … (IV, 288–90)

This is true majesty for Milton; their nakedness is an index of inner purity and their erect bearing conveys rectitude. Only fallen monarchy, in Milton's view, needs grand and expensive garments. Against the splendid appearances of Charles II in 1660 Milton subversively offers naked humanity as the measure of genuine royalty. Yet even as we recognise Adam and Eve as human like ourselves, we see that they are ideal versions of us, noble innocents that no longer exist:

> in their looks divine
> The image of their glorious maker shone … (IV, 291–2)

The shining that is in the Son's face, the inner spiritual light, is also theirs.

After stressing the nobility and goodness that is in both equally, Milton turns to gender difference, and here, of course, he is a man of his time, and today's reader is offered something like the picture of domestic hierarchy that had obtained since St Paul:

> … the head of every man is Christ; and the head of the woman is the man … (1 Cor. 11: 3)

Milton offers:

> For contemplation he and valour formed,
> For softness she and sweet attractive grace,
> He for God only, she for God in him:

His fair large front and eye sublime declared
Absolute rule ... (IV, 297–301)

This bald over-simplified statement (that has set feminist hackles in a roar) will be much modified as the relationship between husband and wife deepens; Milton, we discover, is a forward and searching thinker, not simply a traditional one, on gender issues in marriage.

Details of appearance interested him; he was himself as a Cambridge undergraduate 'so faire', says John Aubrey in his *Lives* (compiled in the years following Milton's death and after communicating with Milton's widow), 'that they called him *the lady of Christ's College. Ovall face. His eie a darke gray*'. He had, states Aubrey, 'abroun haire' and 'his harmonicall and ingeniose soul did lodge in a beautifull and well-proportioned body'. Adam has a little of Milton in him but is perhaps more Greek. Milton begins with his head, 'his fair large front and eye sublime', and continues rather with a sculptural than a painterly account of this first ideal man:

> hyacinthine locks
> Round from his parted forelock manly hung
> Clustering, but not beneath his shoulders broad ...
>   (IV, 301–3)

'Hyacinthine locks' had been another hero's, Odysseus's, whose hair 'hung down like hyacinthine petals' (Homer, *Odyssey*, VI, 231), and they suggest less an obvious colour than the shapeliness of Adam's head. They suggest beauty, and we might recall that in Italy Milton had seen many marble testaments to male beauty: statues of the god Apollo. The 'parted forelock', however, was a modern detail borrowed from his own image as we see it in his portraits. He is careful to limit the length of Adam's hair, marking its difference from the Cavalier style of long hair – decadent in Milton's view – worn at the court of Charles II. Eve, however,

> as a veil down to the slender waist
> Her unadornèd golden tresses wore

Dishevelled, but in wanton ringlets waved
As the vine curls her tendrils, which implied
Subjection, but required with gentle sway,
And by her yielded, by him best received,
Yielded with coy submission, modest pride,
And sweet reluctant amorous delay. (IV, 304–11)

From long golden hair covering and half-covering nakedness, Milton moves, unsurprisingly, within the single sentence to sexual attraction, as though he wishes to deal at once with the problem of sexuality before the Fall. For him, there was no problem; unconfined by narrow Puritanism, Milton saw sexuality as a part of unfallen innocent life, man's 'happiest life' (317). Yet throughout his discussion here there runs an awareness of fallen sexuality which shadows the innocence. Eve's tresses are 'unadorned', and so we are compelled to think of the artful adornings that will later complicate natural attraction; they are also 'dishevelled" and her 'wanton ringlets' wave. Her yielding to Adam is with 'coy submission' and she seems to sense her power as she yields with 'sweet reluctant amorous delay.' A hint of sophisticated knowingness is conveyed to us, and we have to make the effort that perhaps Milton intended us to make, to let our minds give back to physical attraction and to the words that evoke it, their original, innocent energy: there is nothing yet of shame in Eve's 'wanton ringlets', 'dishevelled hair' or shy submission. 'So hand in hand they passed' (321), as, hand in hand, still companions, they will finally walk out of the garden and out of the poem, mortals at the end, and sadder and wiser for their experience of losing Paradise.

Here, in Book IV, after 'their sweet gardening labour' (328), 'to their supper fruits they fell' (331). The fruit is to hand, there is no cooking and, having been at work in the garden, they have 'wholesome thirst and appetite' (330). Milton is unusual in that he gives Adam and Eve something to do in their unfallen state: they eat, make love, bring order to the garden, converse together or with an angel, and praise God. Work, in Milton's Puritan ethic, was not merely, as was traditional, a consequence of the Fall; it was a good in itself, and Adam and Eve take their pre-lapsarian gardening seriously. As they eat and rest in harmony, harmony and pleasure surround them: 'all beasts of the earth' gambol before them:

> Sporting the lion ramped, and in his paw
> Dandled the kid. (IV, 343–4)

Milton catches something of the characteristic energy of each animal without its aggression in this scene of the Peaceable Kingdom, wild nature at peace (a favourite subject for artists) before the Fall. The 'serpent sly' is amongst Milton's creatures and it is hard for the reader to feel that this 'insinuating' beast can ever have been quite innocent.

Throughout, Satan has been watching,

> O hell! What do mine eyes with grief behold ... (IV, 358)

He is pierced with pain at the human pair's tenderness and beauty, 'could love' them, 'could pity', but quickly hardens:

> I with you must dwell, or you with me
> Henceforth ... (IV, 377–8)

Dwelling with them he will bring sin into their minds, and his other kingdom, the external hell,

> shall unfold,
> To entertain you two, her widest gates,
> And send forth all her kings; there will be room ...
> (IV, 381–3)

'Honour and empire with revenge' (390) compel him, he says, to destroy their 'harmless innocence'. ' So spake the fiend', comments Milton,

> and with necessity,
> The tyrant's plea, excused his devilish deeds. (IV, 393–4)

Satan begins this phase of his attack by watching even more closely. Down from the tree of life as an animal he joins the animals as they perform before Adam and Eve:

> A lion now he stalks with fiery glare,
> Then as a tiger, who by chance hath spied
> In some purlieu two gentle fawns at play,
> Straight couches close, then rising changes oft
> His couchant watch, as one who chose his ground
> Whence rushing he might surest seize them both
> Griped in each paw ... (IV, 402–8)

This lion and tiger, Satan within them, have all the pent-up ferocity of animals after the Fall, but Adam and Eve, gentle fawns themselves, do not notice.

Adam turns courteously to Eve:

> Sole partner and sole part of all these joys ...

He speaks his acknowledgement of their happiness and God's goodness and (in the hearing of Satan) reminds them both of the one prohibition:

> of all the trees
> In Paradise that bear delicious fruit
> So various, not to taste that only tree
> Of knowledge, planted by the tree of life,
> So near grows death to life, whate'er death is ... (IV, 421–5)

Does the fact that Milton has Adam go over this 'easy prohibition' in his first speech indicate that the prohibition exerted an obsessional attraction? or is it simply that the story needed Satan to overhear this, and thus realise how he might destroy the new-created race? Adam is ready to praise God

> and extol
> His bounty, following our delightful task
> To prune these growing plants, and tend these flowers ...
>   (IV, 436–8)

Eve replies with deference that she has an even greater debt of thanks to pay, for she has and enjoys Adam, 'Pre-eminent by so much odds' (447), and like a lover she recollects how she first saw him. It was on the day of her own creation, her birth, which she, unlike all humans since, can describe,

> That day I oft remember, when from sleep
> I first awaked … (IV, 449–50)

'That day I oft remember'; with such touches Milton gives the impression that Adam and Eve have lived for a period in a state of unfallen innocence. Like Shakespeare – in *Othello* say – Milton can shorten or expand time as his story requires. Taking us now back in time Eve recounts her first experience of life. She awoke to a 'murmuring sound / Of waters' (453–4), a cave nearby from which the sound and the waters issued and spread into 'a liquid plain', a lake, still, 'unmoved / Pure as the expanse of heaven' (455–6). Surrounded by water (birth-waters perhaps? Venus from the sea?), Eve looked into the smooth still lake and it seemed to her another sky. She could not distinguish the world from its reflection, particularly when she saw the pleasing reflection of herself. Innocent as Eve was, are we to discern the merest and quite charming potential for vanity in Eve's delighted gazing? Certainly she desired this image in the water and had remained fruitlessly stretching for it had not an authoritative voice from an invisible source informed her that what she saw and sought was herself,

> but follow me
> And I will bring thee where no shadow stays
> Thy coming … (IV, 469–71)

Following the voice and thus renouncing the narcissism that can lead only to death, Eve 'espied thee', she tells Adam, 'fair indeed',

> yet methought less fair,
> Less winning soft, less amiably wild
> Than that smooth watery image; back I turned …
> (IV, 478–80)

but Adam cried aloud, told her about her making, that she was his flesh, his bone, 'nearest my heart':

> Part of my soul I seek thee, and thee claim
> My other half ... (IV, 487–8)

'Part of my soul'; 'sole partner and sole part' was Adam's first address to Eve, and the soul will remain for Adam inextricably fused with her attractions, almost like an aspect of himself. Eve concludes her memory:

> with that thy gentle hand
> Seized mine, I yielded, and from that time see
> How beauty is excelled by manly grace
> And wisdom, which alone is truly fair. (IV, 488–91)

She has been an apt pupil; she understands the paradoxical nature of their relationship: Adam's 'gentle hand seized' hers; the physical action conveys Adam's mixture of tender yielding and forceful authority. Eve has given way, and now, far from wanting to return to loving her own soft beauty, she loves otherness – Adam; further, she has ascended in the hierarchy of feeling from a love purely of the senses to an appreciation of wisdom, of the abstract, the spiritual, which lodged, Milton believed, rather within patriarchal than female apprehension.

Adam has enjoyed Eve's lively account of her origin, and Eve,

> half embracing leaned
> On our first father, half her swelling breast
> Naked met his under the flowing gold
> Of her loose tresses hid ... (IV, 494–7)

Eve is openly inviting and Adam, delighted,

> Smiled with superior love, as Jupiter
> On Juno smiles, when he impregns the clouds
> That shed May flowers; (IV, 499–501)

The word 'superior' troubles readers of today, for it seems to imply that Adam too earnestly takes on the role of teacher; yet the comparison with Jupiter and Juno lightens it; inevitably Jupiter was physically superior to and above Juno in the clouds which would absorb his falling, generative and erotic showers of rain. The embrace of Adam and Eve continues with kisses. Satan watches, and

> aside the devil turned
> For envy, yet with jealous leer malign
> Eyed them askance ... (IV, 502–4)

He has become a leering *voyeur*, and for the first time in the poem he is referred to as 'the devil':

> Sight hateful, sight tormenting! Thus these two
> Imparadised in one another's arms
> The happier Eden, shall enjoy their fill
> Of bliss on bliss, while I to hell am thrust,
> Where neither joy nor love, but fierce desire,
> Among our other torments not the least,
> Still unfulfilled with pain of longing pines ... (IV, 505–11)

Satan, who has only self-love, cannot love another, cannot ever be 'imparadised', for paradise, like hell, is a condition of mind; while desire, ever unfulfilled, is hell. He turns to possibilities of inciting ambition in Adam and Eve, ambition for knowledge, and thus disobedience and infringement of the prohibition about the tree of knowledge. To this end he explores Eden.

Meanwhile Uriel, angel of the sun, comes down to earth

> On a sunbeam, swift as a shooting star ... (IV, 556)

and he warns the archangel Gabriel, head of the angelic guard for earth's security, that a zealous stripling cherub had come by and flown earthward but that his looks had been 'obscured' with 'passions foul'. Gabriel is alerted and Uriel returns on an evening sunbeam. Milton, still describing a day in unfallen Eden, now takes us through changing lights and sounds from sunset to moonrise. There is a royal grandeur about the clouds that on the sun's 'western throne attend'; the 'bright orb' has been arraying them 'with reflected purple and gold'. One feels that Milton's ability to present the glorious light of the sky is an element behind the tributes to light of the Romantic poets

[78]

and artists; for Wordsworth, brilliance of light has something of Paradise in it: every common sight could be 'apparelled', not 'arrayed' (Milton's verb), but 'apparelled' in celestial light ('Ode: Intimations'); for Wordsworth the evening sky was more than light, and, in an occasional poem recalling his Scottish tour and the light of evening, 'stepping westward seemed to be / A kind of *heavenly* destiny' ('Stepping Westward'); the 'magnificence' of 'purpureal evening' could have a radiance that came 'From worlds not quickened by the sun', from indeed 'Heaven's pomp' (Ode: An Evening of Extraordinary Splendour'). And there are other examples: even for 'atheist Shelley', 'the glow / Of Heaven descends upon a land like thee, / Thou Paradise of exiles, Italy' when 'clouds of rich emblazonry / Dark purple at the zenith' modulate to a 'wondrous hue / Brighter than burning gold' ('Julian and Maddalo'). Of the painter Turner's interest in light (and indeed in Milton) there is no need to speak here. Milton's majestic sky is followed by gentleness:

> Now came still evening on, and twilight grey
> Had in her sober livery all things clad;
> Silence accompanied, for beast and bird,
> They to their grassy couch, these to their nests
> Were slunk, all but the wakeful nightingale;
> She all night long her amorous descant sung;
> Silence was pleased … (IV, 598–604)

Silence was not broken, but happy to lose itself and be displaced by the song of the nightingale, for this is Paradise and there is harmony, not competition; silence and birdsong provide accompaniment and descant. Twilight over, different tones of light appear:

>   now glowed the firmament
> With living sapphires: Hesperus that led
> The starry host, rode brightest, till the moon
> Rising in clouded majesty, at length
> Apparent queen unveiled her peerless light,
> And o'er the dark her silver mantle threw. (IV, 604–9)

In such a nightscape as this the Romantic writers would be equally interested. Milton's verbs are all active; the firmament is alive with energy. There is drama; following Hesperus the evening star, and his company of attendant stars, the moon rises in cloud, but at length, manifestly queen, she unveils, is without cloud, peerless, and, still keeping to the same metaphor of clothing, she 'o'er the dark her silver mantle threw.' Wordsworth tries for similar effects in his 'A Night-Piece': after the continuous cloud over the moon, suddenly there is light and above the viewer's head is 'The clear Moon, and the glory of the heavens. / There, in a black-blue vault she sails along.' Wordsworth's sister Dorothy's Journal entry (25 January 1798) observes the same drama.

Adam suggests that they rest, for

> With first approach of light, we must be risen
> And at our pleasant labour ... (IV, 624–5)

Maintenance of the garden in ordered beauty is an immense task; the arbours require

> More hands than ours to lop their wanton growth ...
> (IV, 629)

Children, in other words, will be needed and Adam and Eve must be fertile as well as industrious. Before they retire Milton has Eve declare her love in a lyric of timeless appeal, a song on a stock theme: that nature is beautiful but without the loved one it is meaningless. The details are general and elemental enough to suit these, the first lovers in the world, and they are appropriate for any lovers. The formal circularity, the elaborate patterning of the sweet changes of nature between morning and night, the repetition of these in variation and in simpler phrases make a shapely whole; simultaneously there is a charming distance between Eve's detailed noticing of the regular returns of moments of time and her conviction that while talking with Adam she forgets all time:

With thee conversing I forget all time,
All seasons and their change, all please alike.
Sweet is the breath of morn, her rising sweet,
With charm of earliest birds; pleasant the sun
When first on this delightful land he spreads
His orient beams, on herb, tree, fruit, and flower,
Glistering with dew; fragrant the fertile earth
After soft showers; and sweet the coming on
Of grateful evening mild, then silent night
With this her solemn bird and this fair moon,
And these the gems of heaven, her starry train:
But neither breath of morn when she ascends
With charm of earliest birds, nor rising sun
On this delightful land, nor herb, fruit, flower,
Glistering with dew, nor fragrance after showers,
Nor grateful evening mild, nor silent night
With this her solemn bird, nor walk by moon,
Or glittering starlight without thee is sweet. (IV, 639–56)

The mounting negatives and quicker rhythms of the second
half of the lyric provide Adam with a ringing declaration of
her love. After an aria so rapt Eve moves immediately from
'glittering starlight' to a more prosaic desire for information
about stars: 'wherefore all night long shine these, for whom
/ This glorious sight, when sleep hath shut all eyes?' (657–8).
Before turning to Adam's suggestions in answer to Eve's intellectual query, it is perhaps of interest to wonder if Wordsworth
borrowed from Eve's lyric voice. That voice in Milton is formal; Wordsworth is a conversational narrator, but yet there are
parallels. Eve evokes her love for Adam by pointing twice to
effects in nature; Wordsworth, in recalling, for example, the
time surrounding the death of his father, presents his tension,
grief, and imaginative recovery, by twice evoking the place
where as a boy he had waited for the horses to take himself and
his brothers home from school. Unexpectedly that Christmas
holiday brought his father's death. Waiting for the horses on a
day 'Stormy, and rough, and wild', the boy had sat

> half-sheltered by a naked wall;
> Upon my right hand was a single sheep,
> A whistling hawthorn on my left ...

Just as Eve's perception of nature would be changed if Adam were not there, so Wordsworth's grievous experience has changed his perception of the objects beside which he had waited:

> And afterwards, the wind and sleety rain,
> And all the business of the elements,
> The single sheep and the one blasted tree,
> And the bleak music of that old stone wall
> The noise of wood and water, and the mist ...
>
> (*Prelude*, 1805, XI, 357–89)

The repetition, with variation, of sheep, tree and wall, has made the ordinary things significant, and Wordsworth can find renewal in them as well as loss, can drink from them 'as at a fountain'. He has learnt from Milton – and he uses the technique more than once – the power of repetition with difference.

At this point in *Paradise Lost*, following Eve's love lyric, Adam does his best with her query about why the stars shine at night when no-one sees them; it is a question that interests Adam too and Milton has him later probe more closely into the workings of the cosmos with the archangel Raphael. An epic poem tries to be comprehensive for its own time, and Milton keeps abreast of contemporary scientific thinking. Here, Adam makes intelligent suggestions: that there might be reasons for the stars' movements which are entirely unrelated to the two human beings in Paradise; the stars go regularly round the earth and, by their very presence, keep chaos at bay,

> Ministering light ...
> Lest total darkness should by night regain
> Her old possession ...   (IV, 664–6)

Then again, he and Eve, he says, are not the only creatures to see the stars and respond to the beauty of their order:

Millions of spiritual creatures walk the earth
Unseen, both when we wake, and when we sleep:
All these with ceaseless praise his works behold ...
(IV, 677–9)

He and Eve know this, for they themselves have heard the

Celestial voices to the midnight air,
Sole, or responsive each to other's note
Singing their great creator ... (IV, 682–4)

The wonderful polyphony of the songs of spirits, like the music of the spheres, can only be heard by the unfallen; ordinary mortals since Adam and Eve have been, myth tells us, deaf to it.

Adam and Eve hand in hand go to their 'blissful bower' where neither 'beast, bird, insect, or worm durst enter' for the bower is, as it were, an extension of their own embracing arms where they are 'imparadised', and its full presence in the poem is a measure of Milton's regard for the centrality of sexual expression within the loving space of marriage. Thus, a non-puritanical approach pervades the description of the bower: nature in the bower takes on the splendour of art:

Iris all hues, roses, and jessamine
Reared high their flourished heads between, and wrought
Mosaic; underfoot the violet,
Crocus, and hyacinth with rich inlay
Broidered the ground ... (IV, 698–72)

God, 'the sovereign planter', made the bower, while Eve 'With flowers, garlands, and sweet-smelling herbs' made it her own. She is 'more lovely than Pandora', writes Milton, 'and O too like / In sad event' (714–6), he exclaims. With Satan so close, the comparison with Pandora is indeed ominous for it recalls a prohibition against inquisitiveness, disastrously ignored and consequently releasing swarming evils into the world. Before lying down under 'open sky', Adam and Eve give thanks and praise to God, and thus an unfallen day in Eden ends; they

> Straight side by side were laid, nor turned I ween
> Adam from his fair spouse, nor Eve the rites
> Mysterious of connubial love refused ... (IV, 741–3)

Eve did not refuse, but Milton does; perhaps wisely, he chooses not to present particular sexual detail: he was a man of the seventeenth century, not of today, and in any event his fallen readers might not – without a disproportionate amount of attention on Milton's part – have been able to discriminate appropriately between unfallen embraces here and the fallen sexual play that will be a factor in Adam and Eve's later relationship. Instead of the 'rites Mysterious', Milton offers in their place a formal pæan to Wedded Love:

> Hail wedded love, mysterious law, true source
> Of human offspring ... (IV, 750–1)

He sees sexual joy in marriage as a civilising power, a basis for ordered society and fitting 'holiest place'. A

> Perpetual fountain of domestic sweets, (IV, 760)

it represents the very opposite of either 'the bought smile / Of harlots' or 'Casual fruition ... court amours / Mixed dance, or wanton mask, or midnight ball / Or serenade which the starved lover sings / To his proud fair ...' (765–70). Milton's ideal love has no connection with love as it was understood at the court of Charles II, or with the artificial demands of courtly love. He again is personally moved and sighs over the sleeping Adam and Eve,

> Blest pair; and O yet happiest if ye seek
> No happier state, and know to know no more. (IV, 774–5)

He wants them to 'know' instinctively, intuitively, that their best happiness will lie in their not being over-curious to 'know' more intellectually. The sounding vowels, 'O', 'No', 'Know', 'Know', 'no', with their ending, 'no more', lay a weight of doom upon the 'blest pair's' likely chances of being 'happiest'.

The angelic guards search Paradise for the suspicious 'stripling cherub' and they find 'whom they sought',

> Squat like a toad, close at the ear of Eve … (IV, 800)

The toad had long had a mixed reputation, tending to evil: it was thought of as poisonous, 'ugly and venomous' in Shakespeare's words (*As You Like It*, II. i. 13), and it had no place in the bower, so close to Eve. In this disguise Satan was

> Assaying by his devilish art to reach
> The organs of her fancy … (IV, 801–2)

The very assumption of the toad's shape is a humiliating descent for Satan, and at the touch of goodness, of an angel's spear, this toad is forced to resume his true physical identity, that of Satan, 'the grisly King'. Book IV ends with a vigorous comic 'flyting' between Satan and the good angels, a to-and-fro hurling of insults such as Milton had been accustomed to in the Commonwealth pamphlet wars. A fight almost develops, and Satan is a terrifying figure: 'His stature reached the sky …' (988); Dorothy Wordsworth remembered this line as she gazed in September 1803 upon the near mountains edging Glencoe in Scotland: they

> were the grandest I had ever seen … majestic in their own
> nakedness … such forms as Milton might be supposed
> to have had in his mind when he applied to Satan that
> sublime expression, 'His stature reached the sky'.
>> (*Journals of Dorothy Wordsworth*, ed. De Selincourt, Macmillan,
>> London 1952, I, 332)

But for the time there is no physical battle. God (whose plan, we know, does not envisage 'such horrid fray' at this point) hangs his scale of justice in the sky, and thus demonstrates to Satan how light he weighs, how impossible it was for him to resist. Satan

> fled
> Murmuring, and with him fled the shades of night.
>> (IV, 1014–15)

INTERLUDE

BY THIS STAGE the reader of this essay on reading *Paradise Lost* has met most of the characters of the poem, or rather most of the personages, for characters as we know them from the realistic novel, scarcely describe the personae of *Paradise Lost*. Satan only, in his tempestuous inner conflict, might qualify. Adam and Eve, still innocent, have marks of general goodness, but they are rather universal ideals than individuals. The reader has yet to meet two of the very greatest seraphim, the Archangel Raphael and the Archangel Michael; but they, as we might expect, will be uncomplicated spokesmen for goodness and for God.

The reader has also met Milton: in his outbursts of feeling and his interruptions to the story; in his extended discussion of his epic aims for the poem at the beginning of Book I, his prayer for inner light at the beginning of Book III; his views, ideas and speculations on a massive range of topics.

The reader has become familiar with Milton's language, his strange formal English in sentence structure and vocabulary, which is both energetic and rhetorical and yet capable of the most delicate nuance and ambiguity. The function of the epic simile is familiar to the reader, who will know now either how to take the gist, or even to coast through Milton's extensive classical, biblical, historical, scientific, geographical, mythical, cosmological references or, more slowly and deliberately, on a second reading perhaps, to find a pleasure in patiently looking up information, and relating it to the narrative.

Knowing all this, the present writer has it in mind (because of the exigencies of space) to move perceptibly more quickly through the remaining books of the poem.

BOOK V

ADAM WAKES AND wakens Eve, who tells him of a disturbing dream:

> Close at mine ear one called me forth to walk
> With gentle voice ... (V, 36–7)

She thought the voice was Adam's, and heard her earlier question about why the stars shine at night answered again, this time with a different explanation:

> heaven wakes with all his eyes,
> Whom to behold but thee, nature's desire, (V, 44–5)

the voice declared, implying that she, Eve, was central to the universe. Seeking the voice, Eve walked in her dream by the tree of knowledge and saw and heard a winged figure addressing it:

> is knowledge so despised?
> Or envy, or what reserve forbids to taste?
> Forbid who will, none shall from me withhold
> Longer thy offered good, why else set here?
> This said he paused not, but with venturous arm
> He plucked, he tasted; me damp horror chilled ... (V, 60–5)

But when the winged being went on to extol the virtues of the fruit and point out that Eve could

> be henceforth among the gods
> Thy self a goddess, not to earth confined ... (V, 77–8)

she tasted the fruit he held 'even to my mouth' and immediately 'With him I flew and underneath beheld / The earth outstretched immense' (87–8). Suddenly, 'My guide was gone, and I, methought, sunk down, / And fell asleep; but O how glad I waked / To find this but a dream!' (90–3). Eve's relief at waking, at recovering control of her own consciousness is immense. Satan, the toad at her ear, has penetrated her unconsious defences, and Milton has understood that dreams are built partly on one's own waking thoughts, on what lies profoundly beneath them, on wishful (or fearful) extensions of those thoughts and, in Eve's case, upon flattery. This dream, with its sudden flight and exaltation, its sudden humiliation, drop and isolation, is irrational like nightmare, and it is Satan's trial run for the actual temptation; he will use the same psychological techniques.

Adam cannot explain the dream, cannot know what evil is, but he has total confidence in Eve's innocence,

> Evil into the mind of god or man
> May come and go, so unapproved, and leave
> No spot or blame behind. (V, 117–9)

The two are comforted and begin their daily morning hymn of praise to God for the wonders of his creation. Milton makes it clear that they spoke no repetitive memorised prayer or fixed liturgy; their eloquence is spontaneous (perhaps closer to ideal Puritan practice than to that of the established church). Yet their celebration of the creation as a means of knowing God is distinctly reminiscent of, for example, Psalm 148 and the Canticle Benedicite. The psalmist implores everything from the heavens and the angels to the creeping things and flying fowl, all of them individually, to praise the Lord. Milton has all these things not merely praise, but dance their praise, and not separately, but in linked movement. The angels 'with songs / And choral symphonies, day without night, / Circle his throne rejoicing'; those in heaven join with all creatures on earth to 'Extol / Him first, him last, him midst, and without end' (165). The writer of Revelation had God declare, 'I am Alpha and Omega, the first and the last' (Rev. 1: 11); Milton, in his line, slow and sonorous, stresses God's infinite extension in time, a note that Wordsworth took up in his *Prelude* (1805, VI, 572), to describe how all the turbulent, discordant energies of wind and cloud and water, 'Tumult and peace', speak ultimately not only of their vivid bursts of power, but of their opposite, the permanent and the timeless. Milton's line, expanded from Revelation, is expanded again by Wordsworth to indicate that the forceful energies of the natural world are nevertheless

> The types and symbols of eternity,
> Of first, and last, and midst, and without end.
> (*Prelude*, 1805, VI, 555–72)

Adam and Eve in their Hymn seem instinctively to know that the movements of creation give praise to the God that is eternally still. From the circling and singing angels they turn to celebrate the stars, then the sun, that sounds his praise 'both when thou climb'st … and when thou fall'st'. The moon flies with the fixed stars; the planets, 'wandering fires', move 'in mystic dance not without song'; air in its 'ceaseless change' varies its praise; mists rise to the sky:

> Ye mists and exhalations that now rise
> From hill or steaming lake, dusky or grey,
> Till the sun paint your fleecy skirts with gold,
> In honour to the world's great author rise,
> Whether to deck with clouds the uncoloured sky
> Or wet the thirsty earth with falling showers,
> Rising or falling still advance his praise. (V, 185–91)

Rising and falling movements are continuous, as are the winds that 'breathe soft or loud' from the four quarters, the pines that wave their tops and every plant that waves in wind, the fountains 'that warble as ye flow', the birds 'That singing up to heaven gate ascend', the gliding fish and the lowly creeping things. The divine plan reveals the universe's happy interdependence, where the sun makes clouds, that make rain, that feeds the earth, that makes plants. From the insects to the angels there is nothing static in Adam and Eve's reading of the universe, and the created things praise God simply in being themselves, in participating in a world that is alive.

Adam and Eve too are themselves, and it is as natural to them as it is to the earth and its creatures to render praise to the Creator. They too will have a falling and a rising, but theirs cannot remain as inevitable and as joyous as nature's unself-conscious celebration. In a poem very much concerned with rising and falling at all levels, the morning hymn is both an example of innocence in relation to God and will be a powerful reminder of that lost state when Adam and Eve, after their moral and psychological falling, will find that the parallel rising will require effort and endeavour that is so far unknown in Paradise.

> After their prayer,
> On to their morning's rural work they haste. (V, 211)

God 'beheld ... with pity', and asked Raphael to spend 'half this day as friend with friend' (229) with Adam and warn him that 'by deceit and lies' an attempt could well be made upon his happiness,

> Happiness in his power left free to will,
> Left to his own free will ... (V, 235–6)

Raphael, with his six wings of the seraphim, flies down to earth and walks through the 'flowering odours', the 'wilderness of sweets' (293–4); that was Paradise.

It was mid-day, Adam, 'from the heat of noon retired / To respite his day-labour with repast' (231–2), was sitting 'in the door ... Of his cool bower' (300–1), while 'Eve within, due at her hour, prepared / For dinner savoury fruits' (303–4) ('savoury' here means 'appetising'). It is a domestic humanising touch and of course offers an example of what seventeenth-century man – and men of a later date – assumed proper for the conduct of home affairs. The meals Eve prepares would delight a modern dieter: fruits from all over the world are at hand, growing and ripe. For drink, Eve crushes grapes, different berries, and from 'sweet kernels' presses 'dulcet creams'. She heaps the fruits so that tastes will not clash, for 'Tastes not well joined' are 'inelegant' (335). Nothing is cooked in Paradise as there can be no fire until after the Fall, yet Milton has given sophisticated attention to this primitive meal. He could easily have arranged for Raphael to speak with Adam and Eve in some other context, but the meal is important: there is something close to the sacramental in eating with others. Again, Adam and Eve, in extending hospitality to an archangel, demonstrate a sense of their own worth and dignity, and tell us of the sociable closeness to the spirit world that might have been a possibility for all humanity. The shared meal indicates too that Milton believed that immortal angels had corporeal needs: his angels sleep, embrace (we discover), eat. Eating indeed features large in *Paradise Lost*: a banquet in heaven will be balanced by the devils in Hell desperately falling upon fruit that resembles that of the Tree of Knowledge, and finding themselves chewing bitter ashes. And of course the entire drama of the poem, the fall into experience, hangs upon the eating of an apple.

Adam's greeting of his 'godlike guest' was simply his walking forth:

> in himself was all his state,
> More solemn than the tedious pomp that waits
> On princes, when their rich retinue long
> Of horses led, and grooms besmeared with gold
> Dazzles the crowd, and sets them all agape. (V, 352–7)

Adam's state is kingly; Milton, keeping close in a friend's house in 1660 would have heard the cannons and the shouts, and known of the retinue and the grooms besmeared with gold as Charles II entered London. He once again offers a single naked man as the standard of royalty. After the shared meal Raphael, speaking of similarities between man and angel, explains to Adam and Eve that there is a hierarchical ascent from nourishment of the body to expansion of the spirit; he takes a plant as an example: this progresses from root to lighter stalk to airier leaves, last to 'the bright consummate flower' (481), even 'by gradual scale' to 'vital spirits' and thence through animal to intellectual, creating

Fancy and understanding, whence the soul
Reason receives, and reason is her being,
Discursive or intuitive; discourse
Is oftest yours, the latter most is ours [the angels],
Differing but in degree, of kind the same. (V, 486–90)

Raphael points the way:

Your bodies may at last turn all to spirit ...
If ye be found obedient ... (V, 497–501)

This is the nub of it, and Adam is pleased that

In contemplation of created things
By steps we may ascend to God. (V, 511–12)

He wonders how

Can we want obedience then
To him, or possibly his love desert
Who formed us from the dust. (V, 514–16)

At this question, Raphael, fulfilling God's injunction, reminds
Adam of the need for obedience:

that thou art happy, owe to God;
That thou continuest such owe to thyself,
That is, to thy obedience; therein stand. (V, 520–2)

In explaining that hearts are free to choose love and service of
God, and are 'not over-ruled by fate', he comments that it is
just the same for the angels:

freely we serve,
Because we freely love, as in our will
To love or not; in this we stand or fall:
And some are fallen, to disobedience fallen,
And so from heaven to deepest hell; O fall
From what high state of bliss into what woe! (V, 538–43)

At this point Adam begs to know why and how the angels fell
and Raphael tells the story, beginning at the beginning. The

[94]

poem itself, *Paradise Lost*, had begun part way into the story with Satan already defeated, 'hurled headlong' out of heaven, and lying vanquished with his fallen angels in the fiery gulf of hell. Satan's reaction to his defeat is the poem's opening subject and it is told largely from his point of view, his view of himself as mighty rebel against tyrannic authority, as champion of freedom; it is within the shelter of these notions that he catches at the reader's imagination; he becomes for many the first romantic hero. Raphael has perforce a different interpretation. He has to begin earlier, well before the creation of the earth and its universe, a time when

> this world was not, and Chaos wild
> Reigned where these heavens now roll, where earth
> now rests ... (V, 577–8)

In heaven, Raphael recalls, all the angels were assembled, 'Orb within orb' and God announced,

> This day I have begot whom I declare
> My only Son ... (V, 603–4)

(The word 'begot' here means 'made him a king.)

> ... to him shall bow
> All knees in heaven, and shall confess him Lord. (V, 607–8)

(We already know that the Son deserves this distinction for he alone, as we heard in Book III, offers to undergo death for mankind.) At God's announcement there was rejoicing in heaven, song, dance,

> Mystical dance ...
> mazes intricate,
> Eccentric, intervolved, yet regular
> Then most, when most irregular they seem (V, 620–4)

and a banquet in honour of the Son's exaltation. But, continues Raphael, Satan 'could not bear / Through pride', was 'fraught with envy against the Son of God', and he withdrew his legions, marching them all night to his 'quarters of the north', pretending needful preparations for a visit from the Messiah. He took with him 'the third part of heaven's host', and they reached his place, the 'palace of great Lucifer' (760). Here, Satan throws off allegiance and pesuades his followers to cast off 'prostration vile', now doubly required, for Son as well as Father:

> Will ye submit your necks, and choose to bend
> The supple knee? (V, 787–8)

Raphael, telling this to Adam, is clearly giving an account of speeches which he did not hear and describing actions in the north which he did not witness. This seems not to matter, for the relation is as much to the reader as it is to Adam, and the whole flashback, the account of what happened before the story's beginning in Book I, is a convention of epic well within most readers' (and filmgoers') familiarity. Virgil, in a flashback in the *Aeneid*, has his hero Aeneas, comfortable at the time with Queen Dido in Carthage, re-live his pain as he tells her of his terrible experiences at the fall of Troy, and the account helps the reader understand his subsequent desertion of Dido. The flashback in Milton's epic, Raphael's narration to Adam, comes half-way through the poem, takes us out of Eden and into vast stretches of time and space; takes us out of the loving and courteous relationship of Adam and Eve and into the driving envy and jealousy of a bold and powerful figure; takes us from the locality of a garden into confrontation and battle between mighty forces of good and evil. This conflict between good and evil, which will have its individual and psychological manifestation in Eve and in Adam, is of cosmic proportions in heaven, and Raphael has to describe magnitude.

Before the huge battles begin, Raphael speaks of a single angel's personal encounter with Satan and his formidable forces, and the account is no doubt offered to Adam as an instructive example. Raphael is a good teacher; he both tells and shows. He speaks of how in Satan's domain of the north (rebellion has more than once come out of the north – Charles I, no less, had tried in the 1640s to raise an army in the north to oppose Parliamentarian rule and restore monarchal privilege), the seraph Abdiel, one of Satan's angels, 'Stood up ... in a flame of zeal'. To stand up, single, against Satan and his massive host is a heroic act. It is almost a reminder of how Satan himself had come across in the first Books of the poem, the single rebel against authority, the hero who would not admit defeat. Abdiel's standing up is such a moment of theatrical action, but of course it is more: it is at one with the psychic action of Abdiel's whole being, the sustaining in constancy, of loyalty to the service of God; this is the true heroism, and it is this that Milton himself aspired to. Abdiel faces Satan and argues from experience of God's goodness:

> Shalt thou give law to God, shalt thou dispute
> With him the points of liberty, who made
> Thee what thou art? (V, 822–4)

How can Satan assert that Christ's exaltation is merely the unjust elevation of an equal over equals when Christ is the begotten Son, is the Word, and

> by his Word the mighty Father made
> All things, even thee ... (V, 836–7)

Rather it is, points out Abdiel, that godhead has descended, that the Son, seeming equal and submitting himself to Heaven's laws, has thereby exalted the whole community of lesser angels.
  Satan will have none of this:

> who saw
> When this creation was? Remember'st thou
> Thy making, while the maker gave thee being?
> We know no time when we were not as now;
> Know none before us, self-begot, self-raised
> By our own quickening power ... (V, 856–61)

It is an astonishing, even a childish self-assertion; we do not deny our birth because we cannot remember it as Satan here denies his creation by the co-eternal Father/Son. Satan, aspiring to be monarch of heaven, will in fact make himself monarch of hell and his kingship, self-made, must begin by shedding the Father, and repudiating family love. It is a kingship exactly opposed to the divine monarchy which is founded on family love. Against Abdiel's arguments Satan and his hosts remain bold, confidently relying, like certain post-Reformation thinkers of the seventeenth century, solely upon themselves:

> Our puissance is our own, our own right hand
> Shall teach us highest deeds, by proof to try
> Who is our equal ... (V, 864–6)

Abdiel,

> unmoved,
> Unshaken, unseduced, unterrified
> His loyalty he kept, his love, his zeal; (V, 898–900)

'Long way through hostile scorn' (904) he passed, and as Book VI starts he is back among the heavenly host and hearing a voice

> From midst a golden cloud ...
> Servant of God, well done, well hast thou fought
> The better fight, who single hast maintained
> Against revolted multitudes the cause
> Of truth ... (VI, 28–32)

Wordsworth, pondering in 1803–4 on possible subjects for a long poem of his own and briefly discussing such subjects in his *Prelude*, Book I, is clearly at one point searching for an Abdiel figure, a solitary hero,

> I would record
> How in tyrannic times some unknown man,
> Unheard of in the Chronicles of Kings
> Suffered in silence for the love of truth.
>
> *(Prelude,* 1805, I, 201–4)

or how

> ... that one Frenchman, through continued force
> Of meditation on the inhuman deeds

[98]

Of the first Conquerors of the Indian Isles
Went single in his ministry across
The Ocean ... (ibid., 205–9)

Canvassing ideas relating to the solitary hero in the wake of both Milton and his character Abdiel, Wordsworth finally rejects such topics and hits upon his own subject for what is to be *The Prelude*, a subject which yet retains a flavour of Abdiel: the story of his own single engagement with contemporary history and the truth of imagination.

BOOK VI

Without a break Raphael continues his account to Adam of Satan's rebellion. Book VI covers three days of physical battle. 'And there was war in heaven', says the writer of Revelation:

> Michael and his angels fought against the dragon; and the dragon fought and his angels, And prevailed not; neither was their place any more in heaven. (Rev. 12: 7)

Milton uses this but gives Christ the final determining role. The first day's battle is of conventional fighting: squadrons, armour, shields, swords; the second day's is horrific: gunpowder, barbaric violence and the destruction of nature; the third is Christ's total rout of the rebel angels. Why does Milton expand to Book length the War in Heaven? Is he providing the combat scenes that classical writers deemed essential to epic, and at the same time emphasising the childishness of the idea that good and evil can be fought out in physical terms? Why does he not let his all-powerful God conclude the War on its first starting and give goodness the inevitable victory? Is the battle a kind of comic interlude in the intellectual play of good and evil?

It is worth assuming that Milton had a serious purpose. His God arranges that the battle be fair: that the 'armed saints' under Michael be ranged 'by thousands and by millions', 'equal in number to that godless crew / Rebellious' (47–50). We know that Satan drew after him a third part of the Sons of Heaven; there could have been an easy victory over the rebellious had all the loyal angels been conscripted. As readers, we recall the impression given by Satan in Book I of a genuinely dangerous rebellion crushed just in time, of 'dubious battle on the plains of heaven' (I, 104), of a near-equality of strength. This near-equality is now seen in Book VI as a deliberate (and patronising?)

strategy of God's, and the first day's battle ends indecisively. Satan's party fights to take Destiny into their own hands, Michael's party to uphold their free conviction that ultimate Destiny is the province of divine decree; opposition between these two positions is continuous. Meanwhile, fighting without clear supremacy anywhere, Raphael expresses his shock at the fratricide then first beheld:

> that angel should with angel war
> And in fierce hosting meet, who wont to meet
> So oft in festivals of joy and love … (VI, 92–4)

Milton had met this and grieved at it in the Civil War. Abdiel on this first day seeks out Satan, magnificent 'in his sun-bright chariot', 'Idol of majesty divine' (100–101); he continues his previous argument with the rebellious archangel and insists that there is no servitude in serving God:

> God and nature bid the same,
> When he who rules is worthiest, and excels
> Them whom he governs. (VI, 176–8)

Milton himself stood by this belief; in his Second Defence of 1654 he addressed Cromwell who in his view had saved the country: 'We all willingly yield the palm of sovereignty to your unrivalled ability and virtue.' Milton believed in merit. Abdiel's view is that it is not he but Satan who is not free, 'to thy self enthralled' (181). He strikes Satan, knocking him backwards. Immense noise and clashes ensue:

> long time in even scale
> The battle hung … (VI, 245–6)

The battle awaits Michael's single combat with Satan. This is as though

> Two planets rushing from aspect malign
> Of fiercest opposition in mid sky,
> Should combat, and their jarring spheres confound.
>
> (VI, 313–5)

Michael's sword cuts into Satan:

> then Satan first knew pain,
> And writhed him to and fro convolved ... (VI, 327–8)

> and from the gash
> A stream of nectarous humour issuing flowed
> Sanguine, such as celestial spirits may bleed,
> And all his armour stained ere while so bright. (VI, 331–4)

The exciting duel is interrupted while Milton breaks off to tell us about the angelic constitution and its power quickly to heal. Many deeds of prowess were performed, including some by Raphael which Raphael modestly declines to describe, and Milton of course cannot approve such exploits as true epic subject matter. Night falls and Satan rallies his wearied host for the next day's battle.

His followers revive when Satan tells them his plan: he has invented gunpowder. Canons are made and next day, the second day,

> deep throated engines belched, whose roar
> Embowelled with outrageous noise the air,
> And all her entrails tore, disgorging foul
> Their devilish glut, chained thunderbolts and hail
> Or iron globes, which on the victor host
> Levelled, with such impetuous fury smote,
> That whom they hit, none on their feet might stand,
> Though standing else as rocks, but down they fell
> By thousands, angel on archangel rolled; (VI, 586–94)

Satan 'in derision called', but not for long. God's roused angels are in rage:

> They plucked the seated hills with all their load,
> Rocks, waters, woods, and by the shaggy tops
> Up lifting bore them in their hands ... (VI, 644–6)

The rebel angels struggle out from under these hurled hills

> and the neighbouring hills uptore;
> So hills amid the air encountered hills
> Hurled to and fro ... (VI, 663–5)

Heaven is turned into an image of hell, and the whole savage and destructive picture must be for Adam a pattern of what life might be like in a world that is fallen, where the good themselves are corrupted into dark anger, where evil springs up always with new tactics and must be resisted, but can never be resisted conclusively for the conflict is evenly balanced.

And so the second day ends, with the immense forces held in more and more turbulent stasis. God tells his Son that

> in perpetual fight they needs must last
> Endless, and no solution will be found. (VI, 693–4)

But the third day is the Son's:

> Pursue these sons of darkness, drive them out
> From all heaven's bounds into the utter deep:
> There let them learn, as likes them, to despise
> God and Messiah his annointed king. (VI, 715–8)

Satan implied in Book I that he had practically issued a personal challenge to God and put God's power in jeopardy. It is no such thing: God has infinite reserves. The Son tells him that he

> can put on
> Thy terrors, as I put thy mildness on,
> Image of thee in all things; (VI, 734–6)

and he seats himself in the living chariot of God who thus, in the person of the Son, enters the action, but as himself he is, as ever, withdrawn and inviolable. The Son

> onward came, far off his coming shone,
> And twenty thousand (I their number heard)
> Chariots of God, half on each hand were seen ...
> At his command the uprooted hills retired
> Each to his place, they heard his voice and went ...
> (VI, 768–82)

Without divine intervention the third day would have been as inconclusive as the other two: in the later words of John Calvin, 'it is impossible that the soldiers of Christ should have perpetual peace with the world, whose Prince is Satan.' Impossible though it is, the lesson in Book VI for Adam and Eve is that the soldiers of Christ must keep fighting, though knowing that without help, without the Son of God, they can never win.

The rebel angels on the third day 'rallied their powers', 'hope conceiving from despair', 'disdaining flight'. The Son addresses his own host,

> Stand still in bright array ye saints, here stand
> Ye angels armed, this day from battle rest; (VI, 801–2)

Just as for Milton biblical truth must supersede pagan virtue, so historical action in battle as a subject for epic must make way for the intervention of grace, of that element that is beyond history, beyond time. And so the Son 'into terror / Changed his countenance' and

> on his impious foes right onward drove,
> Gloomy as night; under his burning wheels
> The steadfast empyrean shook … (VI, 831–3)

Before the living chariot of lightning, fire and thunder, all the rebel angels were driven

> With terrors and with furies to the bounds
> And crystal wall of heaven, which opening wide,
> Rolled inward, and a spacious gap disclosed
> Into the wasteful deep …
>   headlong themselves they threw
> Down from the verge of heaven, eternal wrath
> Burnt after them to the bottomless pit.
> …
> Nine days they fell …
>   hell at last
> Yawning received them whole, and on them closed.
>   (VI, 859–75)

And we are where we first met Satan and his companions in Book I. God's revenge is terrible; redemptive Love has become ruthless Power as the Son's chariot drives the rebels

> as a herd
> Of goats or timorous flock together thronged ... (VI, 856–7)

Likened to such innocent creatures the fallen angels become almost objects of our pity; such feeling would be misplaced in the theological scheme of things. Christ's wrath – as indeed Milton had seen it portrayed in Michelangelo's *Last Judgment* in the Sistine Chapel in Rome – was not to be underestimated. The Son as Warrior of God conducted his purge of heaven effectively (and Milton had known Purges in Commonwealth politics), not destroying the rebel angels absolutely (for they had a future role to play in the later moral theatre of human choice), but clearing them out of heaven: 'headlong themselves they threw'. Their leaving heaven is not simply passive action; the angels positively threw themselves, and they must illustrate the despair and suicidal tendency to which evil inclines. The Son, God's heir, right hand and war lord, returns into mid-heaven with something like a Roman triumphal entry: all his saints

> With jubilee advanced; and as they went,
> Shaded with branching palm, each order bright,
> Sung triumph, and him sung victorious king ... (VI, 884–6)

Yet even here, at the end of this martial success, this triumph shaded with the branching palm of victory, we are taken out of this epoch belonging to a period before the creation of our world and given a glimpse ahead into future time when the same Son of God, at that future point the God of Love, will ride into Jerusalem on an ass and the people 'Took branches of palm trees and went forth to meet him' (John, 12:13). Even as we see the Son's wrath, we are not allowed to forget his love.

Book VI ends with Raphael reminding Adam that Satan 'envies now thy state' and 'is plotting how he may seduce / Thee also from obedience' (900–902). 'Warn thy weaker', he advises, perhaps a little tactlessly even for the seventeenth century, since Eve is present: 'remember, and fear to transgress' (912). The seventeenth-century reader too might heed this last advice, for all readers of the time were Christian soldiers, and their specific heroic action here was to continue to read to the end of this poem, and like Adam to absorb its meaning.

BOOK VII

THERE IS A new start after the War in Heaven. The second half
of the poem opens with a sense of building afresh, of creativity after the violence of the rebellion, and Milton, as he had
in Books I and III, speaks personally of himself as writer. He
calls on his heavenly Muse for help, since so much 'yet remains
unsung'. He has been writing about affairs in heaven, but from
now the poem will be set firmly on the earth, and it is there
that the Muse must help him:

> Descend from heaven Urania ...

Urania was one of the Nine Muses, the Muse of Astronomy,
but although Milton will describe the heavenly bodies, it is not
primarily in that capacity that he invokes this Muse. Her name,
Urania, means 'heavenly', and it is, as he comments, 'The meaning, not the name I call' (5). His Urania was not the one who
dwelt on 'old Olympus',

> but heavenly born,
> Before the hills appeared, or fountain flowed,
> Thou with eternal Wisdom didst converse,
> Wisdom thy sister, and with her didst play
> In presence of the almighty Father ... (VII, 7–11)

It is a happy family scene; Wisdom was with God before the
Creation and Urania, the heavenly Muse, was with her. A product of Hebraic and Hellenic cultures, she has served Milton
well so far:

> Up led by thee
> Into the heaven of heavens I have presumed,
> An earthly guest, and drawn empyreal air ... (VII, 12–14)

but now the poet must be

> Standing on earth, not rapt above the pole ...

and may possibly be 'more safe' and

> sing with mortal voice, unchanged
> To hoarse or mute, though fallen on evil days,
> On evil days though fallen, and evil tongues;
> In darkness, and with dangers compassed round,
> And solitude; (VII, 24–8)

The constraint upon Milton, blind and a Puritan poet under a Restoration monarchy, can be sensed in these lines where words are emphatically repeated, phrases merely inverted, and the word 'evil' sounded three times; there seems no escape from these very words or from the darkness, dangers and solitude. And Milton was indeed for a time in danger: republican colleagues were hanged, drawn and quartered in the early days of Charles II's reign; perhaps Milton's blindness was seen as punishment enough. The Act of Oblivion of August 1660 ensured his safety. In danger, certainly, as he wrote, yet not in solitude, 'not alone'; Milton corrects himself and again addresses the Muse:

> yet not alone, while thou
> Visit'st my slumbers nightly, or when morn
> Purples the east: still govern thou my song,
> Urania, and fit audience find, though few. (VII, 28–31)

Not alone, for inspiration came to Milton at night; speaking of Hebrew poetry and the strength he drew from it, he had said early in Book III,

> Thee Sion and the flowery brooks beneath
> That wash thy hallowed feet, and warbling flow,
> Nightly I visit: (III, 30–32)

And after nightly visits Milton could dictate. He begs Urania to find 'fit audience' for his song, 'though few'. Milton had to have confidence in the truth of his writing, whether it was pamphlet or poem:

... the truth not smothered, but sent abroad, in the native confidence of her single self, to earn, how she can, her entertainment in the world, and to find out her own readers: few perhaps, but those few, such of value and substantial worth, as truth and wisdom, not respecting numbers and big names, have been ever wont in all ages to be contented with.

(Preface to Eikonoklastes, 1649, 2nd ed., 1650)

The fit audience for *Paradise Lost* is every person who reads it and there are readers, and have been readers, in every age; these admire the poem, argue with it, dislike it, condemn it, interpret and re-interpret it, use, imitate, exploit it constantly. They keep it alive.

For Milton even to finish the poem in those early days of 1660, and for the fit audience to emerge, Urania needed to

> drive far off the barbarous dissonance
> Of Bacchus and his revellers, the race
> Of that wild rout that tore the Thracian bard
> In Rhodope, where woods and rocks had ears
> To rapture, till the savage clamour drowned
> Both harp and voice; nor could the Muse defend
> Her son. So fail not thou, who thee implores:
> For thou art heavenly, she an empty dream. (VII, 32–9)

It was Milton's fear, and particularly his fear in the dark days of the Restoration, that 'the barbarous dissonance' of society was fiercely hostile to the solitary poet, the artist. Artists have often been made aware of society's destructive impulse towards them, but rarely with the intensity of Milton, who saw the Caroline court, 'Bacchus and his revellers', as a deathly force. The fate of the Thracian bard Orpheus, the mythic poet who could enchant woods and rocks, had been a powerful presence in Milton's elegy of 1637, *Lycidas*, written in memory of a minor Cambridge poet, Edward King, drowned at sea. Orpheus' fate was worse than drowning: it was dismemberment and then drowning by Dionysiac frenzied women wild with meaningless noise, a savage killing of poetry; and there was no help:

> What could the muse herself that Orpheus bore,
> The muse herself for her enchanting son
> Whom universal nature did lament,
> When by the rout that made the hideous roar,
> His gory visage down the stream was sent,
> Down the swift Hebrus to the Lesbian shore.
>
> (*Lycidas*, 58–63)

The muse, Calliope, could not defend her son; Milton has better hope, for his Muse, Urania, is 'heavenly', Calliope, pagan, 'an empty dream'. This is important to Milton; mastery of one's art is not enough to save a man; Orpheus was the greatest master of music and poetry; Bellerophon, whom Milton also cites in this passage, was a great rider and could ride the winged horse Pegasus – but he had not Jove's protection, and Jove sent a gadfly to sting the horse and throw Bellerophon to his death. Milton, beyond his mastery, has to implore the far greater protection of God's divine power and the inspiration of divine knowledge. He trusts that with this he can bring about a new creation in the remaining books of *Paradise Lost*.

And he begins in Book VII with the Creation itself. We hear, before Raphael turns to this, how attentive Adam and Eve had been to his account of Satan's rebellion,

> things so high and strange, things to their thought
> So unimaginable as hate in heaven,
> And war so near the peace of God in bliss ... (VII, 53–5)

Addressing Raphael as 'Divine interpreter' Adam, in courteous epic tradition, begs the story-teller to tell them more, and to tell them, if it is not forbidden, about God's 'eternal empire', 'the more / To magnify his works, the more we know' (96–7). Raphael is agreeable, for knowledge, he says, 'is as food', and his comment is surely not without some irony as we recall that Eve and then Adam will fatally take as food the fruit of the tree of good and evil, the tree of knowledge. The food Raphael offers here is appropriate knowledge, but he will have to speak of God's thoughts and acts, and he indicates that to human ears these things 'Cannot without process of speech be told, / So told as earthly notion can receive' (178–9). Milton's readers are used to this, for this is how, inevitably, the angelic war of Book VI was told – in terms that historical mortal readers would understand. It is a way too of allowing Milton to write myths to explain what he himself as a mortal could have no conception of. God's instantaneous acts of creation are therefore told, as they are in Genesis, as a six-day story.

God announces that through the medium of the Son he will undertake the Creation, not in the least because he needs to; Satan has not 'dispeopled heaven', and angelic forms will not as such replace the fallen hosts. Simply, and in a moment, God will create something different,

> Another world, out of one man a race
> Of men innumerable, there to dwell,
> Not here, till by degrees of merit raised
> They open to themselves at length the way
> Up hither, under long obedience tried,
> And earth be changed to heaven, and heaven to earth,
> One kingdom, joy and union without end. (VII, 155–61)

This is his will; his goodness, he explains,

> is free
> To act or not, necessity and chance
> Approach not me, and what I will is fate. (VII, 171–3)

His happy plan of heavenly 'union without end' must of course be a non-starter, and it conveys the difficulties some readers can have with *Paradise Lost* if they want the poem to be logical, reasonable and consistent. But then Christian theology is far from logical.; we know from Genesis itself, from two thousand years of history, from the very first line of Milton's own poem, that the cheerful scenario God envisages here will not happen; God knows that man will fall, but knows that he will have every freedom to fall or not fall, and he knows that the beautiful world he is about to create will be spoilt. Wonderfully, none of this is alluded to, and Book VII becomes one of the purely happy books, perhaps the only entirely happy book, in *Paradise Lost*. Or is even this pæan to creation and to nature darkened for the reader, since we read it immediately after reading Book VI where the destructive passions of fallen (and good) angels and their violent actions are but too recognisable and too like the destructive violence of fallen men in history.

Be that as it may, Book VII, free of the actions of either mortals or immortals, is a happy book and the first result of God's declaration of his will is rejoicing in heaven. The angels sing:

> Glory they sung to the most high, good will
> To future men, and in their dwellings peace ... (VII, 182–3)

These angels sang spontaneously as 'the morning stars sang together' when God laid, he told Job (38: 7), the foundations of the earth at the Creation; or as the multitude of the heavenly host at the Incarnation, that later moment of a new Christian creation, when they sang of Glory to God in the highest, and on earth peace, good will toward men (Luke 2: 14). There is continual harmony right through the six days of the Creation, from the time when 'heaven opened wide / Her ever during gates' to let out the Son in his chariot; even as the golden hinges of the gates moved there was harmonious sound, and each day's act of making, from 'Let there be light' to the creation of Adam, becomes an act of worship as the angels shout and sing and touch their golden harps

> and hymning praised
> God and his works, creator him they sung. (VII, 258–9)

The vision of becoming that is Book VII begins when the Son

> took the golden compasses, prepared
> In God's eternal store, to circumscribe
> This universe, and all created things:
> One foot he centred, and the other turned
> Round through the vast profundity obscure. (VII, 225–9)

God is an architect, an inventor, an artist, as he brings into being an orderly cosmos far removed from 'the loud misrule / Of Chaos' (271–2). The act of creation is an act of energy:

> Immediately the mountains huge appear
> Emergent, and their broad bare backs upheave
> Into the clouds, their tops ascend the sky:
> So high as heaved the tumid hills, so low
> Down sunk a hollow bottom broad and deep,
> Capacious bed of waters: (VII, 285–90)

Mountains are born; they upheave themselves. Milton's verbs indicate the joy of becoming and of having identity:

> Rose as in dance the stately trees, and spread
> Their branches hung with copious fruit; or gemmed
> Their blossoms ... (VII, 324–6)

The sun was 'made porous to receive / And drink the liquid light, firm to retain / Her gathered beams' (361–3). The animals, fish, flesh and fowl, teem and swarm; the sky is filled with wings; on the sea 'bended dolphins play' and under the green wave shoals of fish

> Graze the sea weed their pasture, and through groves
> Of coral stray ... (VII, 404–5)

They

> Show to the sun their waved coats dropped with gold,
> Or in their pearly shells at ease, attend
> Moist nutriment, or under rocks their food
> In jointed armour watch: (VII, 406–9)

Everywhere the essential nature of the creatures becomes clear, as here where fish watch their food, or as the lion seizes its energetic nature even as it emerges from the earth to become itself:

> The grassy clods now calved, now half appeared
> The tawny lion, pawing to get free

His hinder parts, then springs as broke from bonds,
And rampant shakes his brinded mane; (VII, 463–6)

No creature, however small, is undeserving of mention: the ant is presented along with the symbolism later attached to it:

> First crept
> The parsimonious emmet, provident
> Of future, in small room large heart enclosed,
> Pattern of just equality perhaps
> Hereafter ... (VII, 484–8)

Whatever the value, in Milton's view, of the ant as a model for human society, God has made an ideal natural commonwealth of the earth; it is fertile and bursting with plenitude, yet not out of control. We do however register the size of the task that will face Adam and Eve and their future offspring; already our two parents find it hard to manage the profuse plant growth of their secluded garden in Eden. Here we see that at the Creation God's original plan for nature embraced both the teeming activity of the earth and its order and harmony; the elements, earth, air and water, are appropriately and decorously used:

> earth in her rich attire
> Consummate lovely smiled; air, water, earth,
> By fowl, fish, beast, was flown, was swam, was walked
> Frequent ... (VII, 501–4)

The triple elements, the creatures in triplicate, their movements also in a threesome, perfectly conclude a satisfactory creation.

It is now the sixth day, when

> he formed thee, Adam, thee O man
> Dust of the ground, and in thy nostrils breathed
> The breath of life; in his own image he
> Created thee, in the image of God
> Express, and thou becamest a living soul. (VII, 524–8)

The pauses here in the first line emphasise Adam's individuality – his name; point to his being general universal man, 'O man';

and point to his origin and to his end, 'Dust of the ground'. There is feeling in the frequent voicing of the words 'thee', 'thy', 'thou', in the intimate way God 'in thy nostrils breathed / The breath'; this echoing language, with the word 'image' imaging 'image', convinces us that Adam was indeed created 'in the image of God'. Milton would know too Michelangelo's own tender concept of the half-reluctant releasing from God's hand of his own beautiful new created Adam that is painted on the ceiling of the Sistine Chapel. Eve, at this point in the poem, is more perfunctorily created 'for race'; the two are exhorted by the Son to be fruitful and multiply; the prohibition about the tree is explained; 'in the day thou eat'st, thou diest; / Death is the penalty imposed' (544–5), and the Son leaves earth at the close of the sixth day. Angelic harmonies again accompanied:

> Open, ye everlasting gates, they sung,
> Open, ye heavens, your living doors; let in
> The great creator from his work returned
> Magnificent, his six days' work, a world;
> Open, and henceforth oft ... (VII, 565–9)

Again the triple pauses emphasise grandeur: 'Magnificent, his six days' work, a world' and Milton's variation on Psalm 24's 'And the king of glory shall come in' offers a full answer to the Psalmist's question, 'Who is this king of glory?'. Book VII answers that the king of glory is the great creator. Destruction has given way to Creation, and God is magnified not for his power to revenge, but for his power of original creation. This is true kingship.

> Who can impair thee, mighty king, or bound
> Thy empire? (VII, 608–9)

sing the angels.

It all depends upon Adam.

BOOK VIII

ADAM AND EVE at the beginning of Book VIII (which, in the first edition of 1667, was the final part of Book VII) still sit in rapt attention as Raphael brings to an end his high blaze of lyrical narrative describing the Creation:

> what recompense
> Equal have I to render thee, divine
> Historian ... (VIII, 5–7)

asks Adam, as nevertheless he moves further into Raphael's debt by desiring the divine Historian to tell him more.

> When I behold this goodly frame, this world ... (VIII, 15)

he begins, not as Hamlet falling into the rhythms of despair, but in a spirit of inquiry, and he wonders why all the 'numbered stars' seem 'to roll / Spaces incomprehensible ... merely to officiate light / Round this opacous earth' (19–23). This is the very question, though its tone is more intellectual, that Eve had asked Adam in Book IV: why do the stars shine at night? Eve sees now that Adam is about to enter upon 'studious thoughts abstruse' and so she

> Rose, and went forth among her fruits and flowers,
> To visit how they prospered, bud and bloom,
> Her nursery; they at her coming sprung ... (VIII, 44–6)

Like Venus in her highest mode, Eve is in herself a creative principle and at her touch the flowers 'gladlier grew'. It is not that she would not have understood or been delighted at Raphael's discourse, Milton hastens to explain, but that she would prefer to hear the arguments from Adam's lips, with his caresses intermixed: the discussion of the old earth-centred system (Ptolemaic), or the newer sun-centred (Copernican), or

Raphael's speculation that the earth itself might give off light, might to the moon 'be as a star'. Raphael clearly enjoys the speculative play but he has no firm answers; how could he have, product as he is of a mortal poet? From whatever stand one stood there was danger in being too bold; Milton himself had

> found and visited the famous Galileo, grown old, a
> prisoner to the inquisition, for thinking in astronomy
> otherwise than the Franciscan and Dominican licensers
> thought.
>
> *(Areopagitica: a Speech for the Liberty of Unlicensed Printing*, 1644)

Raphael's speculations range freely, and Milton, himself an independent thinker, clearly encourages intellectual inquiry in the state of innocence, but perhaps because precise facts about astronomical matters were not possible in the seventeenth century, the whole discussion of the heavenly bodies strikes the reader as one of Milton's images for the limitation of human (or indeed angelic) knowledge. Raphael reminds Adam that the heavens are indeed 'as the book of God ... / Wherein to read his wondrous works' (67–8), but not obsessively to search out their every and most remote secret. These,

> From man or angel the great architect
> Did wisely to conceal ... (VIII, 72–3)

and after much speculation of his own Raphael directs Adam back to his proper concerns:

> Solicit not thy thoughts with matters hid,
> Leave them to God above, him serve and fear ...
> Dream not of other worlds, what creatures there
> Live ... (VIII, 167–76)

Adam has enjoyed the intellectual flight and now contentedly agrees that

> to know
> That which before us lies in daily life,
> Is the prime wisdom ... (VIII, 192–4)

He offers however to tell Raphael his own story and thus retain longer his great guest. Raphael is pleased, for when Adam was created, he feels bound to explain, 'I that day was absent, as befell' (229); he had been on guard at the gates of hell to see that no newly-fallen spirit escaped to disturb the work of creation. The flashback is thus meticulously, even absurdly, fitted into the plot, and Milton has Adam tell how he came to consciousness, 'As new waked from soundest sleep' (253). For Eve, remembering her own first day (IV, 449–90), it had seemed that from sleep she too first awaked.

'Straight toward heaven', says Adam,

> my wondering eyes I turned,
> And gazed a while the ample sky, till raised
> By quick instinctive motion up I sprung,
> As thitherward endeavouring, and upright
> Stood on my feet … (VIII, 257–61)

All Adam's instinct is upwards towards the heavens, while Eve, we recall, 'bent down to look' into smooth water and was dangerously close to an infatuation with her own image. Adam then observes the 'Creatures that lived, and moved, and walked, or flew' (264). He says that

> all things smiled,
> With fragrance and with joy my heart o'erflowed.
> (VIII, 265–6)

Those two nouns, 'fragrance' and 'joy', one abstract and of the senses, the other also abstract and concerned with mood, come together in the heart and we are convinced of Adam's overwhelming pleasure at the world about him. He looks at himself and has his first thoughts, which are of origin and identity:

> But who I was, or where, or from what cause,
> Knew not; to speak I tried, and forthwith spake …
> (VIII, 270–1)

With his new and absolute command of language, he instinctively first addresses the sun, that light that stands so often for divine goodness, and after that the earth and the creatures, and begs to be told, 'how came I thus, how here? / Not of my self; by some great maker then ... / Tell me, how may I know him, how adore' (277–80). (Satan, we recall, had declared himself self-begot.) Nor does Adam's coming into being, his birth, promote the self-contemplation that so engrossed Eve initially; Adam has a religious instinct. He needs to know

> From whom I have that thus I move and live,
> And feel that I am happier than I know. (VIII, 281–2)

He needs to know so that he can praise, and this in Milton's view – and in the view of Christian thinkers since St Augustine – is the true justification for seeking knowledge. Wordsworth, a hundred and fifty years later, in middle age, must have recalled Adam's spiritual hunger to know his 'great maker', for he echoes Milton's line:

> Enough ...
> if, as tow'rd the silent tomb we go,
> Thro' love, thro' hope, and faith's transcendent dower
> We feel that we are greater than we know.
> (From the conclusion to *The River Duddon* sonnet sequence)

Wordsworth inevitably has to lay stress on hope and on faith's mystery rather than its certainty, for he has not unfallen Adam's advantage that he can know the reality of God by conversing with him in the Garden of Eden.

That conversation takes place after Adam, calling out to discover his maker, searching for a father, straying here and there, sinks into sleep

> untroubled, though I thought
> I then was passing to my former state
> Insensible, and forthwith to dissolve ... (VIII, 289–91)

In sleep he dreams, and in the dream a guide 'of shape divine' takes him 'over fields and waters, as in air / Smooth sliding without step' (301–2) to the woody mountain, the high garden with walks and bowers, with trees 'Loaden with fairest fruit':

> whereat I waked, and found
> Before mine eyes all real ... (VIII, 309–10)

He was in Eden. This transporting of Adam to the ideal place via a dream was later, in 1817, seized on by the young Keats, who used Milton's notion to demonstrate the power of the Imagination: 'The Imagination', wrote Keats to Benjamin Bailey, 'may be compared to Adam's dream – he awoke and found it truth.' Adam, waking in Eden, is about to start his wandering and searching again when the 'Presence divine' that had been his dream-guide appeared from among the trees, and

> Whom thou sought'st I am
> Said mildly ... (VIII, 316–7)

and so God and Adam begin their conversation. Paradise is Adam's, says God, 'to till and keep' and of its fruit to eat freely, with the exception of the fruit of that one tree

> which I have set
> The pledge of thy obedience and thy faith ... (VIII, 324–5)

In no uncertain terms is Adam told of the consequences of disobedience: death, and expulsion into 'a world of woe and sorrow'. The 'rigid interdiction', relates Adam, 'resounds / Yet dreadful in mine ear' (334–5), and this despite his ignorance of what precisely death was. As in Genesis Adam gives names to 'the fowl of the air and to every beast of the field' (Gen. 2: 20). Milton, carefully excluding fish, has the creatures approach 'two and two',

> I named them, as they passed, and understood
> Their nature ... (VIII, 352–3)

God is showing Adam that man is indeed lord of the created world. As in the old tale of Rumpelstiltskin, power comes through naming, and beginning with this ritual God and Adam together establish male dominance over language, nature, and ultimately woman.

The creatures, two by two, 'lion with lioness', bring home to Adam however his own lack:

> In solitude
> What happiness, who can enjoy alone? (VIII, 364–5)

Milton's God seems to take something of a humorous interest in Adam's discomfiture and reasonably points out that there is no solitude when all the creatures are

> at thy command
> To come and play before thee, know'st thou not
> Their language and their ways, they also know,
> And reason not contemptibly; (VIII, 371–4)

Whatever communicative powers animals had before the Fall, Adam is not comforted; he expresses a loneliness that perhaps only intense Protestants could know, those who wrestled alone with themselves and with God. He continues,

> Among unequals what society
> Can sort, what harmony or true delight? (VIII, 383–4)

He is seeking fellowship, 'fit to participate / All rational delight' (390–1). Clearly, he sees the true end of language as rational conversation, and although he has never seen another human being he knows that he needs a companion. The creation of Eve is not initially associated with the need for progeny but with Adam's need for an intellectual equal. Milton stresses this and has God delay Eve's creation until Adam can articulate this need from his own experience; it is the beginning of society. And so God continues to test and tease Adam, asking him to consider God's own position,

> Who am alone
> From all eternity, for none I know
> Second to me or like, equal much less. (VIII, 405–7)

Adam humbly puts it to God that he, God, is perfect, and cannot have that desire for 'conversation with his like to help, / Or solace his defects' (418–9). Nor has God need to 'propagate, already infinite'. Adam has thus, in dialogue, been brought to define his view of relationship, and of course he has expressed

Milton's view of ideal marriage. Certain therefore of Adam's right feeling, God reveals that he has planned for Adam's contentment all along:

> I, ere thou spakest,
> Knew it not good for man to be alone ...
> What next I bring shall please thee, be assured,
> Thy likeness, thy fit help, thy other self,
> Thy wish exactly to thy heart's desire. (VIII, 444–51)

Overwhelmed by sudden sleep, yet conscious and in a dream-like trance, Adam sees the glorious shape he has been speaking with stoop and take a rib from him, shape it, and form a creature

> Manlike, but different sex, so lovely fair ... (VIII, 471)

And so Eve is born, from man; her origin and dependence are from man. The Book of Genesis, the Church over hundreds of years, Milton, all offer the same explanation of woman. Milton's additional insistence upon Adam's primary need for the rational companionship of an equal, is all the more important in view of the power of this old and limited biblical myth.

Having thus established that the new companion is both dependent upon Adam and an independent rational equal, Milton can then enjoy, along with the reader, Adam's new feelings: the rushing ecstasy of love as it is experienced for the first time. Adam feels, even in his dream, that the new creation

> infused
> Sweetness into my heart, unfelt before ... (VIII, 474–5)

But then she disappeared and, said Adam, 'left me dark'. He woke into a sense of loss but soon saw the real woman coming towards him, guided by God's voice. She is to him uniquely his own, the child, like Athene of Jove, of a male parent only. Adam speaks aloud his gratitude to the 'Giver of all things fair' and declares his oneness with this new extension, this aspect of himself,

> I now see
> Bone of my bone, flesh of my flesh, my self
> Before me ... (VIII, 494–6)

Delighting in the memory of his first wooing of Eve, Adam continues the account to Raphael of his joy, speaking all the more freely perhaps in that Eve was not present to hear her praises. Milton had arranged for her to be occupied with her flowers while Adam was trying to sort out his feelings. Raphael, we discover later, listened with some disquietude.

As he cried out in gratitude, Adam recalls, and declared that he and the new creature called woman should be 'one flesh, one heart, one soul' (499), Eve heard his voice, saw him and turned away. Adam remembers this correctly: Eve herself had said, 'back I turned' when she described her own first sight of Adam (IV, 480); she had been turning back to that soft desirable image in the water, her own reflection. Adam – and perhaps Milton too – prefers a different interpretation: the seventeenth-century male pleasure in seeming female reluctance, the turning away that was then deemed proper to 'innocence and virgin modesty'.

> To the nuptial bower
> I led her blushing like the morn ... (VIII, 510–11)

and Adam follows this with a marriage song, a Prothalamion, in which everything honours the consummation, from the 'happy constellations' to the earth, to each hill and the joyous birds:

> fresh gales and gentle airs
> Whispered it to the woods, and from their wings
> Flung rose, flung odours from the spicy shrub,
> Disporting, till the amorous bird of night
> Sung spousal, and bid haste the evening star
> On his hill top, to light the bridal lamp. (VIII, 515–20)

The celebration is active: the breezes ('fresh gales') and the soft winds ('gentle airs') whisper it to the woods, and their very whispering is musical, for these winds, in that play upon a word that Milton loves, are airs as well as air, and though gentle they have busy wings, 'Flung rose, flung odours ...'; it as though the invisible perfume of the rose could become as substantial as the rose itself and be flung before the bridal pair. Adam observes that his other pleasures of the senses, his joy in herbs, fruits, flowers, his walks, his sense of taste, of smell, cannot approach this new exquisite feeling for Eve:

> transported I behold,
> Transported touch; here passion first I felt,
> Commotion strange, in all enjoyments else
> Superior and unmoved, here only weak ... (VIII, 529–32)

Of course the creation of Eve brings Adam new problems, new complexities. He worries, using the word 'weak', that he may be deficient in some way to be so transported. His biblical (and his seventeenth-century) ideology tells him that she is 'the inferior, in the mind / And inward faculties',

> yet when I approach
> Her loveliness, so absolute she seems
> And in her self complete, so well to know
> Her own, that what she wills to do or say,
> Seems wisest, virtuousest, discreetest, best;
> All higher knowledge in her presence falls
> Degraded, wisdom in discourse with her
> Looses discountenanced, and like folly shows; (VIII, 546–553)

He finds in Eve 'greatness of mind' and 'nobleness'. Raphael 'with contracted brow' seizes upon Adam's word 'transport',

> what transports thee so,
> An outside? Fair no doubt, and worthy well
> Thy cherishing, thy honouring, and thy love,
> Not thy subjection: weigh with her thy self;
> Then value: (VIII, 567–71)

He recommends the cultivation of self-esteem and reminds Adam that joy from 'the sense of touch whereby mankind / Is propagated ... is the same vouchsafed / To cattle and each beast' (579–82). The distinction Raphael makes is the popular Renaissance one between sacred and profane love, or love and irrational passion. Reason is the key:

> love refines
> The thoughts, and heart enlarges, hath his seat
> In reason, and is judicious, is the scale
> By which to heavenly love thou mayst ascend,
> Not sunk in carnal pleasure ... (VIII, 589–93)

Adam, writes Milton, is 'half abashed'; yet he clearly feels, and Milton with him, that he does not fully deserve this reprimand. He has, he says, 'mysterious reverence' for the 'genial bed', but more than that, delight for

> those graceful acts,
> Those thousand decencies that daily flow
> From all her words and actions mixed with love
> And sweet compliance, which declare unfeigned
> Union of mind, or in us both one soul; (VIII, 600–4)

They share soul as well as body, and in addition, declares Adam with dignity, he is free to 'Approve the best, and follow what I approve' (611). There is a grand simplicity in Adam's account of human love; Milton seems to be expressing the ideal that he was fighting for in his Divorce pamphlets.

The conversation between the archangel and the human ends with Adam's desire to know from Raphael what place there is for love in the angelic hierarchy. How do angels express love?

> by looks only, or do they mix
> Irradiance, virtual or immediate touch? (VIII, 616–7)

'Thou know'st / Us happy', replies the angel blushing, 'and without love no happiness' (620–1). Angels are spirits, and can embrace 'Easier than air with air'. Their union is perfect, 'Total they mix'. As such they have everything that human lovers have, but simply in perfection without the conveyancing of 'flesh to mix with flesh, or soul with soul' (629). That Milton includes a discussion of what one might call gendered love in heaven raises sexual love to heights of spiritual possibility and stresses yet again Milton's belief that sexuality has a place in the world of innocence.

With the setting sun Raphael prepares to leave. He repeats his advice,

> take heed less passion sway
> Thy judgment to do aught, which else free will
> Would not admit …
> … stand fast; to stand or fall
> Free in thine own arbitrament it lies. (VIII, 635–41)

They part, and Raphael goes

> up to heaven
> From the thick shade, and Adam to his bower. (VIII, 652–3)

Book VIII ends with the thick shade of evening. Raphael's now distant account of the War in Heaven and of the Creation, Adam's discussion with him about his own birth, his conversation with God, his love for Eve, have placed at a remove the envious and destructive passion of Satan towards earth's inhabitants. But the poem, the early part of the story now told and the flashbacks over, must return to Satan's consuming hatred. The thick shade of evening will not be enough for Adam, and before another day is done he will wish for the deepest darkness.

BOOK IX

MILTON BEGINS AGAIN. His reader is at last ready for the long promised account

> Of man's first disobedience, and the fruit
> Of that forbidden tree, whose mortal taste
> Brought death into the world, and all our woe,
> With loss of Eden ... (I, 1–4)

Those are the first words of the poem, and they are echoed at the start of Book IX. There can be no more familiar talk with angel guest:

> I now must change
> Those notes to tragic; foul distrust, and breach
> Disloyal on the part of man, revolt
> And disobedience: on the part of heaven
> Now alienated, distance and distaste,
> Anger and just rebuke, and judgment given,
> That brought into this world a world of woe ... (IX, 5–11)

The hammering negatives bring back the poem's initial tone of doom: 'distrust', 'Disloyal', 'disobedience', 'distance', and a 'distaste' that looks back in a condemnatory pun to the 'mortal taste' of Book I. There is no mention here, as there was in Book I, of a Redeemer, 'till one greater man / Restore us' (I, 4–5). The notes, Milton tells his reader plainly, are now tragic, and we are again reminded that Milton's first intention, certainly by 1640, was to write a play, a tragedy on the theme of Paradise Lost: four drafts exist, outlining variously the persons and the action of the projected drama. Book IX itself, dealing with the climax of the poem, has a tragic and dramatic structure: it has a limited cast of characters, a single place as its setting, a short time for the action to be fulfilled, a scene showing the result of action and a choric narrator. And it is part of an epic or heroic story, whose subject 'pleased' Milton, 'long choosing, and beginning late' (26). His chosen subject, he asserts, is 'more heroic than the wrath / Of stern Achilles' (14–15), or the rage of any other Homeric or Virgilian leader in

> Wars, hitherto the only argument
> Heroic deemed ... (IX, 28–9)

(One could argue that Milton nevertheless thought it worthwhile to include wars in his epic, the wars in Heaven of Book VI, while simultaneously deeming these in some of their aspects closer to mock-heroic than to heroic.) Milton rejects also, as an epic subject, 'joust and tournament', with all its 'tinsel trappings' and 'gorgeous knights', and will keep to his own 'higher argument' if his Muse, his 'celestial patroness', will help him. She

>   deigns
> Her nightly visitation unimplored,
> And dictates to me slumbering, or inspires
> Easy my unpremeditated verse: (IX, 21–4)

With such help, he confides to his reader, his poem will not only be heroic (epic), but will 'raise that name' – presumably to heights epic has not yet known – unless a hostile fate should intervene,

>   an age too late, or cold
> Climate, or years damp my intended wing
> Depressed ... (IX, 44–6)

He begins as it were the first Act of his tragic book. Its single character is Satan, whom we almost have to get to know afresh, encountering again the formidable fallen angel who seeks revenge upon Adam and upon Eve for his own infinite loss. The flashback containing Raphael's account of Rebellion and Creation and Adam's life-story has claimed the reader's attention and put at a distance Eve's distress at that dream of temptation and fall that Satan gave her, 'squat like a toad' close at her ear (IV, 800 and V, 30–93). Forced to flee (at the end of Book IV) for 'seven continued nights ' (IX, 63), Satan circled the earth, finally re-entering Paradise, unseen by 'cherubic watch'. Milton has him move underground with the River Tigris and then 'involved in rising mist' rise up in a fountain inside the garden and by the tree of life (72–5), a destructive power penetrating to the very root of being. Now, roaming the earth, Satan settles on the 'serpent subtlest beast of all the field' (86) to be his 'fittest imp of fraud' (89). From north to south, from east to west, the beauty of the earth has struck him, 'O earth, how like to heaven …' (99), he begins, and Milton allows him a long impassioned soliloquy which serves to remind the reader of conflicting aspects of Satan that we have met before: his responsiveness to beauty, his sense of exclusion, his determination to destroy, 'only in destroying I find ease' (129); his pride that

> I in one night freed
> From servitude inglorious well-nigh half
> The angelic name … (IX, 140–2)

his confusion as to whether God made man because he 'failed / More angels to create, if they at least / Are his created' (145–7), adds Satan, perhaps remembering that he had declared the angels self-begot; his shame,

> O foul descent! That I who erst contended
> With gods to sit the highest, am now constrained
> Into a beast, and mixed with bestial slime,
> This essence to incarnate and imbrute,
> That to the height of deity aspired; (IX, 163–7)

his awareness that

> Revenge, at first though sweet,
> Bitter ere long back on itself recoils; (IX, 171–2)

his jealousy and envy of 'this new favourite / Of heaven, this man of clay' (175–6). Satan's mode of speech is already that of fallen man; we all recognise his 'if only' syntax:

[133]

> With what delight could I have walked thee round,
> If I could joy in aught, sweet interchange
> Of hill, and valley, rivers, woods and plains,
> Now land, now sea, and shores with forest crowned,
> Rocks, dens, and caves; but I in none of these
> Find place or refuge; (IX, 114–9)

Here is our all too familiar conditional clause of wish and impossible fulfilment and the 'but' of harsh reality. Satan enters the serpent, trying out the incarnation – 'This essence to incarnate and imbrute' – an incarnation so different from the Son's, and one that will later be forced upon him.

Within the serpent he waits and the second 'act' of Book IX begins. There are two characters, Adam and Eve. Morning dawns, and after the morning's orisons, the two discuss their plans for the day. This is a domestic scene in a domestic setting: there are no angelic hosts or great cosmic spaces in Book IX. The drama is human. 'Till more hands aid us', Eve points out, their 'pleasant task' is overwhelming; what they lop or prune 'grows / Luxurious by restraint' (208–9). This is only to be expected but does Eve, one wonders, over-value efficiency when she suggests that they separate and work in different parts of the garden, he 'where most needs' and she to 'yonder spring of roses intermixed / With myrtle' (218–19). In such division their customary 'casual discourse' and loving ways would not impede the work. 'Sole Eve, associate sole', begins Adam courteously,

> Well hast thou motioned, well thy thoughts employed …
> … for nothing lovelier can be found
> In woman, than to study household good … (IX, 229–33)

Yet this seventeenth-century husband feels that there is nothing to censure in the 'sweet intercourse / Of looks and smiles' (238–9) and he is confident that their 'joint hands' will serve at least to 'keep from wilderness' the paths 'as wide / As we need walk' (244–6). Still, trying to see Eve's point, and with perhaps a rueful remembrance of her earlier declaration, 'With thee conversing I forget all time' (IV, 639), he voices a sudden insecurity,

> if much converse perhaps
> Thee satiate, to short absence I could yield.
> For solitude sometimes is best society,
> And short retirement urges sweet return. (IX, 247–50)

He stresses the word 'short', reminds Eve of the warning concerning the 'malicious foe', and begs her,

> leave not the faithful side
> That gave thee being, still shades thee and protects.
> (IX, 265–6)

Eve replies in tones of 'sweet austere composure'. The sweetness covers an ominous determination; Milton is analysing the dynamics of a seventeenth-century marriage, possibly any marriage where the woman needs to show that she is self-sufficient, that she is the man's intellectual equal, that she feels restricted by his authority. Eve tells Adam that she is thoroughly aware of the devil's threat: Adam himself had informed her of it and she had overheard the archangel Raphael's final words. She is hurt that Adam fears

> that my firm faith and love
> Can by his fraud be shaken or seduced;
> Thoughts, which how found they harbour in thy breast
> Adam, misthought of her to thee so dear? (IX, 286–9)

Eve's indignation is in her breathless tortuous syntax, and Adam immediately replies 'with healing words', addressing his wife with all dignity:

> Daughter of God and man, immortal Eve … (IX, 291)

pointing out that 'Subtle' that enemy 'needs must be, who could seduce / Angels' (307–8); he tactfully confesses his own dependence on Eve, for were he approached and she with him,

> shame, thou looking on,
> Shame to be overcome or over-reached
> Would utmost vigour raise …

[135]

> Why shouldst not thou like sense within thee feel
> When I am present … (IX, 312–6)

Milton is demonstrating his belief that even in an ideal relationship, a relationship before the Fall, the two people are individuals, have differences and need to express these. Eve retains her 'accent sweet' and argues that they cannot dwell thus 'In narrow circuit straitened by a foe' (323). Essentially she takes up Milton's argument from his *Areopagitica* (1644):

> I cannot praise a fugitive and cloister'd virtue unexercised and unbreathed, that never sallies out and sees her adversary.

Of course, she is right, and it is she, not Adam, who first launches on the course of individualism. Already in her dream she has had an experience different from Adam's. They must both realise that they are separate entities, and that their learning must be a process of trial – which may of course involve error. Adam can only point out that for man,

> within himself
> The danger lies, yet lies within his power:
> Against his will he can receive no harm.
> But God left free the will … (IX, 348–51)

He declares that not mistrust,

> but tender love enjoins,
> That I should mind thee oft, and mind thou me. (IX, 357–8)

Rather desperately, he even tries authority:

> Wouldst thou approve thy constancy, approve
> First thy obedience; (IX, 367–8)

but then in sheer tenderness he suddenly capitulates, making it impossible now for her to decide to remain with him:

> Go; for thy stay, not free, absents thee more;
> Go in thy native innocence … (IX, 372–3)

Eve goes, but having gained her point there is a half reluctance to her going

> … from her husband's hand her hand
> Soft she withdrew … (IX, 385–6)

The hands seem to wish to stay joined and the verb of parting, 'withdrew', comes late and softly after the soft togetherness. But Eve goes, as she must, for the issue has been the delicate one of freedom and responsibility. The protector must cease to protect for the child to grow, and for Eve to become the fully mature adult, she must have the freedom to know danger, as indeed must Adam. Milton, within the give and take of dialogue, has tried to show how hard and how necessary it is to find a balance between independence and possessiveness. He adds a further complexity by showing that Adam reaches his decision to agree to Eve's desire to work alone not only on philosophical grounds but on the grounds of his own anxiety that he should rank high in Eve's view of him. In a way he abandons his own reasonable judgement that he should be with her at all costs.

Eve goes, 'like a wood-nymph light / Oread or dryad, or of Delia's train' (386–7). These mountain or wood nymphs could live only as long as their own trees; they were not immortal. Eve will shortly resemble them; she will not long be 'Immortal Eve'. But before this happens, in a cluster of comparisons rising in intensity and beginning with the nymphs, Milton, citing goddesses of classical myth, chooses to give us a final reminder of Eve's beauty and her innocence in an innocent world. She surpassed Delia (Diana) in 'goddess-like deport' and bearing, although not armed with the fierce 'bow and quiver' of that chaste goddess of hunting, but charmingly

> with such gardening tools as art yet rude,
> Guiltless of fire had formed, or angels brought. (IX, 391–2)

She was like Pales, the goddess of pastures, or Pomona, the divine spirit of fruit trees, or Ceres, the goddess of corn and agriculture,

> Ceres in her prime,
> Yet virgin of Proserpina from Jove. (IX, 395–6)

In that line and a half Milton evokes an immense story of innocence, loss and grief which carries ominous parallels with Eve's troubled future and her imminent Fall, for Ceres came to know sorrow as she searched the world for her daughter, Proserpina, kidnapped and forced to live with the king of the underworld. Eve goes, and Adam

> Her long with ardent look his eye pursued
> Delighted, but desiring more her stay.
> Oft he to her his charge of quick return
> Repeated, she to him as oft engaged
> To be returned by noon amid the bower ... (IX, 397–401)

Here, Milton, with a compassionate exclamation, enters again the world of his poem:

> O much deceived, much failing, hapless Eve,
> Of thy presumed return! Event perverse!
> Thou never from that hour in Paradise
> Found'st either sweet repast, or sound repose; (IX, 404–7)

He laments that Eve will be a victim of deception (or self-deception?); that she will fail in some way; that she will simply be unlucky, 'hapless Eve'. Act II of Book IX's tragic structure ends here, and our response to the event perverse, the temptation of Act III will grow in complexity as Eve becomes more like us.

Satan and Eve are the protagonists. Eve and the garden have never seemed more beautiful than they do just before the Fall when 'the fiend / Mere serpent in appearance' comes upon the flower-like woman amongst her flowers. His long seeking for the human pair has covered Paradise place by place, ending in a lengthy sentence which moves steadily to its object, phrase by phrase. This is the final part of the 17–line sentence:

> He sought them both, but wished his hap might find
> Eve separate, he wished, but not with hope

Of what so seldom chanced, when to his wish,
Beyond his hope, Eve separate he spies,
Veiled in a cloud of fragrance, where she stood,
Half spied, so thick the roses bushing round
About her glowed, oft stooping to support
Each flower of slender stalk, whose head though gay
Carnation, purple, azure, or specked with gold,
Hung drooping unsustained, them she upstays
Gently with myrtle band, mindless the while,
Her self, though fairest unsupported flower,
From her best prop so far, and storm so nigh. (IX, 421–33)

The snaking sentence moving and coiling over 'hap' and
'hope', 'wished' and 'wish', 'separate', 'spies' and 'spied' glances
from Eve stooping to support each flower, to herself as fairest
unsupported flower, her beauty veiled in a cloud, but a cloud
of fragrance. She is not defended. Like a flower scattering its
seeds to contingency, her beauty and energies are exposed, and
she, mindful of the garden's need, is mindless of her own. Satan
is enchanted:

Much he the place admired, the person more. (IX, 444)

Milton gives Satan some respite as he looks at Eve who is as
sweet and fresh to his sight as is a summer morning's walk in the
country to a dweller 'long in populous city pent'. Momentarily
for Satan it is as though the annoyance of sewers might give
way to the smell of grain, or tedded grass, or kine or dairy, and
if, in this epic simile 'fair virgin pass, / What pleasing seemed,
for her now pleases more' (452–3). The assumption behind the
simile is the pastoral convention that hell is like the city, that
the country is innocent, and with Satan lurking in the main
narrative there is the implication that the city-dweller might be
all too likely to take advantage of the country girl's innocence.
Momentarily, however, Satan, 'the evil one[,] abstracted stood /
From his own evil, and for the time remained / Stupidly good'
(463–5). It is a fleeting moment, and we see Satan as pitiful; he
has come to seduce and he is himself seduced, though briefly,

into goodness. But the hot hell always burns in him and he recognises that such pleasure is 'not for him ordained'; fallen angels, though initially they had anticipated enjoyment from the new-created earth, will never obtain it, for purity and evil cannot combine to bring pleasure. Satan is taken aback by his own susceptibility, 'Thoughts, whither have ye led me ...' (473), and so begins the attack.

He approaches Eve. A serpent, he is a splendid image of aspiration, a towering epitome of pride, and he moves, not 'prone on the ground as since', but, like his egotism, on the firm basis of himself:

> on his rear,
> Circular base of rising folds, that towered
> Fold above fold a surging maze, his head
> Crested aloft ... (IX, 497–500)

He

> Curled many a wanton wreath in sight of Eve,
> To lure her eye ... (IX, 517–8)

Satan's flattery, his lies, his entangling rhetoric are all prepared for by the folds and mazes of his appearance and movements. Eve scarcely notices at first for every beast is 'more duteous at her call, / Than at Circean call the herd disguised' (522–3). The reader already knows that Satan-within-the-serpent is the supreme tempter, and this amalgamation of devil and the 'subtlest beast of all the field' (560) is original to Milton, and is far more formidable than the serpent-only tempter of Genesis. The reader is then suddenly launched forward by the Eve/Circe comparison to the idea of Eve herself as a snare, and particularly a sexual snare. This is a strand in our conception of Eve, and doubtless a strand in Milton's conception too; she has to confront the tempter alone. Milton has convincingly arranged that she be alone. The Protestant has to wrestle most with temptation when solitary, for the devil is both outside oneself and inside, and the merest hint of Circe in connection with

Eve takes account of this frightening psychological possibility, that the devil is in part inside.

Satan's very first words to Eve are from the language of courtly love,

> Wonder not, sovereign mistress, if perhaps
> Thou canst, who art sole wonder ... (IX, 532–3)

The two of them begin a kind of flirtation in words, Satan, the skilled orator, producing elaborate compliments, pointing out that Eve's beauty (like the earlier matter of the shining stars at night) is simply wasted:

> one man except
> Who sees thee? (And what is one?) who shouldst be seen
> A goddess among gods, adored and served
> By angels numberless ... (IX, 545–8)

The goddess idea is only passingly touched on here, and Eve wonders how the serpent came to speak. Satan seizes his cue and recounts his lowly serpent story of tree, fruit, hunger, the reaching for the apples (the first time the fruit is so identified in *Paradise Lost*), the resulting ability to think and speculate (not praise God), to speak, to appreciate the beauty of Eve and know the worship due to her,

> Sovereign of creatures, universal dame. (IX, 612)

Satan, in other words, pretends personal experience and gives false testimony. Eve has no means of detecting the falseness and she asks to see this wonderful tree.

> To whom the wily adder, blithe and glad,
> Empress, the way is ready ...
> Lead then, said Eve. He leading swiftly rolled
> In tangles ... (IX, 625–32)

'Lead us not into temptation' is the Prayer Book's hope, while Eve, who had rejected the guidance of Adam, follows the tangles of a flattering serpent. Hope elevates and brightens the serpent crest,

> as when a wandering fire ...
> Which oft, they say, some evil spirit attends
> Hovering and blazing with delusive light,
> Misleads the amazed night-wanderer from his way
> To bogs and mires, and oft through pond or pool,
> There swallowed up and lost, from succour far.
>
> (IX, 634–42)

Lucifer, the great light-bearer, the morning star, his light di-minished, is, in this simile, reduced to a mere delusive will-o'the-wisp that lures country folk to disaster. And lures Eve. When they reach the tree, Eve is firm, even jaunty:

> Serpent, we might have spared our coming hither,
> Fruitless to me, though fruit be here to excess ...
>
> (IX, 647–8)

She tells the serpent of the prohibition, clearly knows it, and knows the consequences of disobedience. She was not igno-rant; she was, as God had said, 'sufficient to have stood'.

But the serpent, often now referred to by Milton as 'the tempter', indignant as it were on Eve's behalf, 'new part puts on'. He becomes even more flamboyantly the actor:

> As when of old some orator renowned
> In Athens or free Rome, where eloquence
> Flourished, since mute ... (IX, 670–2)

(There is no eloquence, Milton implies, in Restoration England.) In fast impassioned rhetoric, asking himself ques-tions and answering them as fast, giving all the appearance of logic, giving Eve no time to reply, Satan removes Eve's fear of disobeying, speaks of disobedience as a 'petty trespass' that will rather excite God's praise for her 'dauntless virtue' (courage); he makes her sceptical of the reality of death, 'whatever thing death be'; and evil, 'why not known, since easier shunned?'

> Why then was this forbid? Why but to awe,
> Why but to keep ye low and ignorant ...

>   ... ye shall be as gods ...
>   ... as gods, since I as man,
> Internal man ...
> So ye shall die perhaps, by putting off
> Human, to put on gods, death to be wished ...
> Goddess humane, reach then, and freely taste. (IX, 703–32)

It is a relentless onslaught, and Eve, knocked about by rhetoric, and unused to finding flaws in logic, has no chance to consider any of the points Satan makes – as, for example, does one have to experience evil in order to know and shun it? She had no suspicions, no means of finding out hypocrisy, no way of knowing that the serpent's 'autobiography' was false; she is blinded by the absurd flattering phrases about 'gods', and even allows Satan's final, bold, absurd, and patently improper address, 'Goddess humane ...'. Satan has kindled her desire for self-sufficiency and worship. Adam is not in her thoughts. She gazes at the fruit, desires it sensually and hungrily for its smell; and pauses. Milton has Eve muse within herself, and in her own slower rhythms she parrots Satan's rhetoric, asking herself the same questions about knowledge, good and evil, death, the serpent's experience, 'he hath eaten and lives', God's motives, and suddenly the solution seems simple:

> Here grows the cure of all, this fruit divine,
> Fair to the eye, inviting to the taste,
> Of virtue to make wise: what hinders then
> To reach, and feed at once both body and mind?
>   So saying, her rash hand in evil hour
> Forth reaching to the fruit, she plucked, she ate:
>   (IX, 776–81)

She needs to know empirically: 'she plucked, she ate', and everything henceforth will be history. She has established history. All before was repetition, pleasant indeed and varied enough, and containing elements of learning, but repetition nevertheless. The repercussions begin as the act changes nature:

> she plucked, she ate:
> Earth felt the wound, and nature from her seat
> Sighing through all her works gave signs of woe,
> That all was lost. Back to the thicket slunk
> The guilty serpent ... (IX, 781–5)

Eve does not notice; she is intent,

> nor was godhead from her thought.
> Greedily she engorged without restraint,
> And knew not eating death: (IX, 790–2)

Milton gives us her first thoughts on ceasing to gorge, and they are the thoughts of one 'heightened as with wine'. She addresses the tree reverently, promising to give praise each morning; there is no thought of the accustomed morning hymn to God. The pagan tendency continues as 'dieted by thee I grow mature / In knowledge, as the gods who all things know' (803–4). This is a new and vague theology, and Eve begins to move away from faith, attempting to base her world on, 'next to thee [the tree]', Experience, 'best guide ... thou open'st wisdom's way'. Perhaps the euphoric experience of breaking the tabu makes Eve feel that the tree has real transforming power, that there is a magic about it. As Eve muddles her way into new thoughts and feelings, Milton seems to suggest strongly that no wisdom can be conferred by any eating or drinking; there are no short cuts. His Puritan sensibility, for example, could not approve the High Church ceremonies of Archbishop Laud or the long-held sacramental properties of bread and wine. Much of the remainder of *Paradise Lost* will be about the slow and painful attempt, based on human effort, to deserve again the gift of grace. Eve, meanwhile, at the tree, caught up in new experience, continues to feel herself powerful, even imagining that God, now referred to as

> Our great forbidder, safe with all his spies
> About him ... (IX, 815–6)

has not seen her flagrant trespass. She begins to think of Adam, and to see their relationship for the first time in terms of a political power-structure: should she even tell Adam or 'keep the odds of knowledge in my power', and

> render me more equal, and perhaps,
> A thing not undesirable, sometime
> Superior; for inferior who is free? (IX, 823–5)

Unfallen, she had not of course noticed any inferiority; fallen, she sees that relationships are complicated. Leaving this, and quickly moving to the thought that God quite possibly had seen her, that she might well die,

> And Adam wedded to another Eve,
> Shall live with her enjoying, I extinct;
> A death to think. Confirmed then I resolve,
> Adam shall share with me in bliss or woe:
> So dear I love him, that with him all deaths
> I could endure, without him live no life. (IX, 828–33)

Her jealousy is human, as is her love, and human too is the basic self-regard that informs her thinking and feeling. Primitive in religion now, and offering a low reverence to the tree 'as to the power that dwelt within', she turns her steps towards Adam.

The temptation of Adam is the subject of 'Act IV', and Milton moves to Adam's waiting for Eve's 'return, so long delayed' (844). He has made a garland for her, 'As reapers oft are wont their harvest queen' (842), and the agricultural simplicity of the image reminds us that Eve so recently has seemed more beautiful than 'Ceres in her prime'. Adam sets off to meet her, for his heart, 'divine of something ill, / Misgave him'. Eve, with a bough of fruit in her hand, is flushed when they meet, and her words tumble out in excuse, apology and explanation. She first says, 'Thee I have missed, and thought it long, deprived / Thy presence' (857–8); yet, occupied as she was with the serpent, she seemed scarcely to be thinking of Adam. She rushes to tell him of the tree and the serpent, and says that the fruit will 'open eyes, and make them gods who taste', yet as she tells her story she re-structures her experience and motives, speaking of

> growing up to godhead; which for thee
> Chiefly I sought, without thee can despise. (IX, 877–8)

And we know that she had debated even about telling him! Finally, she puts it to Adam that if he does not taste, she might then 'too late renounce / Deity for thee, when fate will not permit' (884–5).

It is fantasy, and Adam,

> amazed,
> Astonied stood and blank, while horror chill
> Ran though his veins, and all his joints relaxed;
> From his slack hand the garland wreathed for Eve
> Down dropped, and all the faded roses shed: (IX, 889–93)

How often has this scene be played. The lover waits, prepares something special for the beloved; she is late or does not come or comes, as here, but seems a different person. Adam stands silent, careless of his gift, his hand slack and the roses of his garland, unnoticed, have faded and dropped in an instant. Unfallen as he is he does not recriminate, but within himself speaks his sorrow,

> How art thou lost, how on a sudden lost,
> Defaced, deflowered, and now to death devote? (IX, 900–1)

Eve the flower is deflowered and the sexual suggestion is not amiss for she has been seduced by Satan's malicious art – and in some versions of the myth there is literally sexual seduction between Eve and the serpent. Adam however has no hesitation. The

> enemy hath beguiled thee, yet unknown,
> And me with thee hath ruined, for with thee
> Certain my resolution is to die;
> How can I live without thee, how forgo
> Thy sweet converse and love so dearly joined,
> To live again in these wild woods forlorn? (IX, 905–10)

Adam falls, not with thoughts of godhead and self, as did Eve, but for love, a love that will involve his death. It is the sublime of romantic love, and though we know that it is God that he should love most, we love him for his human love of Eve, and care little that he might be considered already partly fallen in that his human love is so intense; without the love and 'sweet converse' of Eve, the beautiful garden will be to him 'these wild woods forlorn'. Another rib shaped into another Eve would not serve,

> no no, I feel
> The link of nature draw me: flesh of flesh,
> Bone of my bone thou art, and from thy state
> Mine never shall be parted, bliss or woe. (IX, 913–6)

It is as fine a reaction as it is immediate, and Adam is calm when he speaks to Eve,

> Submitting to what seemed remediless ... (IX, 919)

Milton cannot change the story of humanity's movement into history and individual responsibility, and the Fall must be Adam's as well as Eve's, but that the situation 'seemed remediless' opens, perhaps mischievously on Milton's part, possible unexplored remedies: a discussion of the situation with God? An offer to die himself instead of Eve? A divorce? Repentance? No intellectual alternatives are considered by Adam; they do not occur to him. It 'seemed remediless', and he calmly goes through Eve's account of the serpent's rise to thought and speech and the possible 'proportional ascent' that might be their own lot, 'to be gods, or angels demi-gods' (937). He tries to argue away the mortal consequences of the 'bold deed' presumed by 'adventurous Eve', and decides that God will hardly 'uncreate' mankind, 'us his prime creatures'. Ultimately, beyond any argument however, he has only one position,

> I with thee have fixed my lot,
> Certain to undergo like doom, if death
> Consort with thee, death is to me as life;
> So forcible within my heart I feel
> The bond of nature draw me to my own,
> ... to lose thee were to lose my self. (IX, 952–9)

The 'bond of nature' may weigh a trifle more heavily here than the earlier 'link', but Adam, in Eve's view, has triumphantly passed the most demanding of courtly love tests,

> O glorious trial of exceeding love ... (IX, 961)

and her words unconsciously invite us to see Adam's sacrifice in relation to what we know of that greater, indeed greatest sacrifice to come. Eve's elevated feelings lead her to envisage a rival sacrifice of her own (surely unlikely) when, if she really were to think death a threat, she would die alone, she declares, protecting Adam from eating the fruit. But she is confident otherwise:

> On my experience, Adam, freely taste,
> And fear of death deliver to the winds. (IX, 988–9)

So, knowing exactly what he was doing, Adam

> scrupled not to eat
> Against his better knowledge, not deceived,
> But fondly overcome with female charm. (IX, 997–9)

And so the blaming begins. Milton himself sets it off here; it will fall upon both, but more heavily upon the woman. In the short space before the mutual recriminations start, the effects of this completion of the Fall are spelled out. On the earth the impact is huge:

> Earth trembled from her entrails, as again
> In pangs, and nature gave a second groan,
> Sky loured and muttering thunder, some sad drops
> Wept at completing of the mortal sin
> Original ... (IX, 1000–4)

Earth's pain is like childbirth and the thing born is 'mortal sin / Original' (1003–4). Adam 'took no thought, / Eating his fill'; Eve joins him and eats again. They are

> As with new wine intoxicated both
> They swim in mirth, and fancy that they feel

> Divinity within them breeding wings
> Wherewith to scorn the earth: (IX, 1008–11)

Flying, having wings, is one of the several motifs of the dream Satan had given Eve (IV, 800 and V, 35–92), motifs that are echoed in the actual temptation: in the dream the winged creature plucked the fruit, held it intimately 'even to my mouth', and after Eve's tasting they had flown together above the outstretched earth. As Eve and Adam in earnest eat the fruit their Fancy of Divinity and wings is as delusive as Eve's dream flight; their Divinity is 'Carnal desire inflaming', and with 'lascivious eyes ... wantonly repaid ... in lust they burn' (1013–15). Adam makes an inviting speech to Eve full of a meaningful suggestiveness and a repellent levity, his wit based upon their recent indulgence in forbidden fruit; he praises Eve's elegant 'taste', 'sapience', 'judicious palate', 'savour', 'true relish'. He ends,

> But come, so well refreshed, now let us play ... (IX, 1027)

This 'play' is the very opposite of innocent play; it is heavy with the same kind of sexual meaning that the jealous obsessional Leontes in *The Winter's Tale* gives it in his third use of the word in the line

> Go play, boy, play. Thy mother plays, and I ...
> (*The Winter's Tale*, I. ii. 187)

Shakespeare's shocking contrast between childhood innocence and fallen experience through the use of the one word 'play' in a single line, could well lie behind Milton's echoing contrast between unfallen love-making, Eve's 'sweet reluctant amorous delay' of Book IV, and the rhyming 'amorous play' after the Fall, where Eve's 'eye darted contagious fire', Adam 'seized' her hand and 'led her nothing loth' to a nearby shady bank. We have to register the difference between this and the earlier 'thy gentle hand / Seized mine, I yielded ...' (IV, 488–9). Milton guides the reader:

> they their fill of love and love's disport
> Took largely, of their mutual guilt the seal,

The solace of their sin, till dewy sleep
Oppressed them, wearied with their amorous play.

(IX, 1042–5)

Thus this first love-making after the Fall is associated with guilt, as sexual activity so often is, and as it certainly was in the punitive theological world of the seventeenth century. It is Milton's brave originality that he insisted on sexual love as a great good; for him, taking a heretical line, sexuality was a part of Adam and Eve's life before the Fall (and for fallen humanity it still could have a high place in a good marriage).

'Act V' of Book IX is brief; it presents an unresolved quarrel between Adam and Eve after they wake from a sleep 'grosser' than they had known and 'with conscious dreams / Encumbered' (1050–1). 'And the eyes of them both were opened', says the writer of Genesis, 'and they knew that they were naked'. They know more than that in Milton: 'their minds / How darkened' (1053–4). Milton compares them both with Samson who wakened after betrayal by Dalilah, 'Shorn of his strength' and knowing shame. Adam and Eve wake

destitute and bare
Of all their virtue: silent, and in face
Confounded long they sat, as strucken mute …

(IX, 1062–4)

Adam finally begins the accusation, making a bitter pun upon Eve's name (which means 'life'):

O Eve, in evil hour thou didst give ear
To that false worm … (IX, 1067–8)

… our eyes
Opened we find indeed, and find we know
Both good and evil, good lost, and evil got,
… naked thus, of honour void,
Of innocence, of faith, of purity,
Our wonted ornaments now soiled and stained …

(IX, 1070–6)

His estrangement from God is terrible to him:

> How shall I behold the face
> Henceforth of God or angel, erst with joy
> And rapture so oft beheld? Those heavenly shapes
> Will dazzle now this earthly, with their blaze
> Insufferably bright. (IX, 1080–4)

God is Light, and Adam now wants only to creep away, to hide, almost to be buried in darkness. His animal cry for retreat is an impulse of despair,

> O might I here
> In solitude live savage, in some glade
> Obscured, where highest woods impenetrable
> To star or sunlight, spread their umbrage broad
> And brown as evening: cover me ye pines,
> Ye cedars, with innumerable boughs
> Hide me, where I may never see them more. (IX, 1084–90)

The depth of his shame and regret is measured by this desperate plea to get as far as possible from light, either by night or day, star or sunlight; he will need the highest woods, the darkest trees. Behind Milton's wood must be Spenser's Wood of Error where the 'loftie trees … heavens light did hide, / Not perceable with power of any starre' (*Faerie Queene*, I, stanza 7); the difference is that Spenser's Red Cross Knight and the Lady Una went into their wood merely to shelter from 'an hideous storme of raine' and they were indeed hidden from heaven's light greatly to their loss and dismay. Milton's Adam actively wants to find such a wood, wants to be far from the light. Milton makes use of the formidable Latinate words, 'obscured', 'impenetrable', 'umbrage', innumerable', as though these in their weightiness could defend the vulnerable retreating creature; in his overwhelming need he cries out in contrasting simple language, 'cover me … Hide me'. Adam, the civilised companion of Eve, the lover of her 'sweet converse', the genial host, the ranging talker with Raphael, the willing worshipper of the Creator, can see his own future only as savage and solitary.

[151]

He and Eve gather leaves of the Indian fig tree, or banyan tree (not the more familiar small-leaved fruit-bearing fig tree), and they make – Milton uses the word 'sew' – a covering 'to gird their waist'. Their going to the tree is itself a move towards hiding, for the tree's

> bended twigs take root, and daughters grow
> About the mother-tree, a pillared shade
> High overarched, and echoing walks between …
> (IX, 1105–7)

Wordsworth, wanting a darkened place beneath a 'sable roof of boughs' suited to the ghostly celebrations of 'Death the Skeleton and Time the Shadow', uses Milton's ecclesiastical phrase, 'a pillared shade' ('Yew Trees', 20). Wordsworth's shade was beneath a group of yew trees and it had no feel of growing life; even the floor was grassless with 'sheddings from the pining umbrage'. Milton's 'pillared shade' and 'umbrage' brought into Wordsworth's poem the darkness he needed – the spiritual dark of Adam's despair. Adam and Eve 'sat them down to weep' (1121), and Milton in these words calls up the weeping, exile and captivity of the Children of Israel, 'By the rivers of Babylon, there we sat down, yea, we wept, when we remembered Zion' (Psalm 137. 1), and thus he suggests the forthcoming exile of Adam and Eve from Paradise. Adam and Eve weep, but not together; each weeps in a private chaos, where

> understanding ruled not, and the will
> Heard not her lore, both in subjection now
> To sensual appetite, who from beneath
> Usurping over sovereign reason claimed
> Superior sway … (IX, 1127–31)

Reason has been usurped and appetite is in power; in the larger scheme of things it is as though Satan had succeeded in dethroning God. Seventeenth-century idealism is overturned, for instinct should not dominate reason; *cogito ergo sum*, Descartes' encapsulation of Renaissance aspiration no longer holds. Adam blames Eve for her 'desire of wandering this unhappy morn'

(1136); Eve points out that Adam might equally have been deceived, and that moreover she was impossibly confined:

> Was I to have never parted from thy side?
> As good have grown there still a lifeless rib. (IX, 1153–4)

She reproaches him for his liberal attitude:

> why didst not thou the head
> Command me absolutely not to go ...
> Hadst thou been firm ... (IX, 1155–60)

Where is the 'sweet converse' now? Adam is incensed:

> what could I more?
> I warned thee, I admonished thee, foretold
> The danger, and the lurking enemy
> That lay in wait; beyond this had been force,
> And force upon free will hath here no place. (IX, 1170–4)

Eve is wilfully misrepresenting the terms of their relationship: Adam was not a master. He finds himself facing that perennial issue of liberty and control, whether of government and people, parent and child, man and wife. Each blames the other. Book IX ends, as the voices of real and recognisable man and woman spend 'the fruitless hours' in 'mutual accusation'. Milton the narrator echoes here in a darker tone Eve's earlier and fatally over-confident use of the word 'fruitless' as she stood at the tree of knowledge:

> Serpent we might have spared our coming hither,
> Fruitless to me, though fruit be here to excess ...
>
> (IX, 647–8)

BOOK X

THE SCENE WIDENS in Book X. All is known; in heaven there is 'dim sadness' as well as pity; on earth the angelic guards are troubled and leave, protesting their vigilance in defending Paradise. 'Be not dismayed' says God's voice from out his secret cloud, and he tells the assembled angels that their 'sincerest care' could not have prevented what he had known would certainly happen: the flattery and seduction of man, with yet

> no decree of mine
> Concurring to necessitate his fall … (X, 43–4)

Milton's God here, in this book, third from the end of the poem, is as he was in the book third from the poem's beginning; Milton always has in mind the formal balancing of the structure of *Paradise Lost*. The facts that are history in Book X are the facts that were prophecy in Book III, and in both books providential foresight and free will are stressed, inextricable, and in their combination, a mystery. Appropriately, to stress mystery, Milton gives God a voice in *Paradise Lost* but not a visible form as himself; even seraphim cannot see him; he is a brightness, 'Dark with excessive bright', as Book III has it. This may not be a perfect representation of God (what could be?) but it is dramatic enough: the disembodied voice offers authority, and the invisibility offers mystery.

'Mercy colleague with justice' (59) is what God wants for man, and the Son, 'Man's friend, his mediator', will best dispense the necessary judgment. The Son, 'Resplendent all his Father manifest / Expressed' (66–7); simply, he can be seen. He goes to earth, 'destined man himself to judge man fallen' (62). As in Genesis it was in the cool of the day that Adam and Eve heard the voice of God, 'now walking in the garden', and they 'hid themselves among / The thickest trees' (100–1). Milton has to stay close to the Bible here, for that is the basis of his poem; he both keeps and expands the words of Genesis and adds psychological complexity. To God's question, 'Hast thou eaten …', Adam is 'sore beset' and worries himself through a long preamble about whether he should or should not conceal Eve's fault and take on the full responsibility. Finally he reaches the statement that is so simple in Genesis:

> The woman whom thou gavest to be with me, she gave me of the tree, and I did eat. (Gen. 3: 12)

The biblical Adam here is blaming others – the woman, and God who created her. His suggestion that the Creator was at fault is expanded by Milton's Adam:

> This woman whom thou madest to be my help,
> And gavest me as thy perfect gift, so good,
> So fit, so ácceptable, so divine,
> That from her hand I could suspect no ill,
> And what she did, whatever in it self,
> Her doing seemed to justify the deed;
> She gave me of the tree, and I did eat. (X, 137–43)

Like Raphael we note Adam's 'transport', his old customary view of Eve – even in God's presence – as 'divine'; his plangent elegiac tone; and we notice too that Adam does not disclose that he had entire knowledge at the time of Fall that the act was wrong. 'From her hand I could suspect no ill' is an untruth, and it lays the blame upon God and his faulty creation. But Adam is fallen man, and we can too easily understand that he seeks to make excuse. The final single line of simple facts, simple words, and straightforward syntax is powerful after some twenty lines of tortuous language. It is a perfect blank verse line and Milton takes it complete from Genesis:

> She gave me of the tree, and I did eat.

The Son's rebuke is firm and it follows orthodox thinking from St Paul to the seventeenth century (and beyond):

> Was she thy God, that her thou didst obey
> Before his voice, or was she made thy guide,
> Superior, or but equal, that to her
> Thou didst resign thy manhood ... (X, 145–8)

He reminds Adam that Eve was 'made of thee, / And for thee', and that

> to bear rule ... was thy part
> And person, hadst thou known thy self aright. (X, 155–6)

That it was he who should have exerted control should have been clear to Adam as it was to seventeenth-century Milton (this does not compromise Milton's equally clear view expressed elsewhere in *Paradise Lost*, that in situations either domestic or national, where the authority figure is not worthy, obedience then to that authority would be wrong and would mean submission to tyranny).

The Son turns to Eve, and Milton prepares the reader to think of Eve sympathetically; she is 'with shame nigh overwhelmed', is not bold, and, unlike Adam, is not 'loquacious':

> The serpent me beguiled and I did eat. (X, 162)

This is all she says; she too, like Adam, transfers responsibility for her fall, in her case, to the serpent. Milton has taken her famous ten syllables also from Genesis, only changing the word-order slightly to make a more rhythmical blank verse line,

> The serpent beguiled me and I did eat ... (Gen. 3: 13)

The Son then pronounces judgments: he addresses the absent serpent that shall go 'upon thy belly grovelling ... / And dust shalt eat' (177–8), and declares that between the Satan-serpent and the woman

> I will put
> Enmity, and between thine and her seed;

Her seed shall bruise thy head, thou bruise his heel.

(X, 179–81)

The bruise of course will be given at last to Satan, as Milton discreetly points out, by the Son himself, 'son of Mary second Eve',

Even he who now foretold his fatal bruise ... (X, 191)

The judgments on Eve and lastly on Adam are much as Genesis has them: children to be brought forth in sorrow, submission to 'thy husband ... he over thee shall rule' (195–6); for Adam the ground is cursed:

Thorns also and thistles it shall bring thee forth ...

(X, 203)

Milton keeps at times so close to Genesis as to be exact:

In the sweat of thy face shalt thou eat bread ...

(X, 205 and Gen. 3: 19)

Finally, he includes from Genesis the notion of man's origin and end, 'dust thou art, and shalt to dust return' (208). But that return to dust will not be immediate; death is deferred.

Meanwhile, the Son,

pitying how they stood
Before him naked to the air, that now
Must suffer change ...
As father of his family he clad
Their nakedness with skins of beasts, or slain,
Or as the snake with youthful coat repaid ... (X, 211–18)

Doing his own Father's bidding, the Son has become the father of his family, and wishes to moderate Adam and Eve's humili-ation, to give them comfort. The first judgment of sin has thus become the first occasion of sin's repair, for love follows the judgment. Milton even has a reference forward to Christ's washing of the disciples' feet, and in this way he suggests the distant incarnation and atonement. That the Son used the skins

[158]

of slain beasts to shield his naked humans from the worsening weather indicates in passing that harmony among the creatures no longer obtains, and beast kills beast. The Son clothed their inward as well as their outer nakedness, arraying them 'with his robe of righteousness' so that they were 'covered from his Father's sight' (222–3). It as though the Father and the Son present two aspects of fatherhood – stern justice and love.

Milton's language in Book X is plain and sober. Adam and Eve are fallen, and the austere language reflects the new conditions. The Son with 'swift ascent' returns to heaven and the reader of *Paradise Lost* moves to the scene at the gates of hell still wide open and

> belching outrageous flame
> Far into chaos, since the fiend passed through ...
> (X, 232–3)

Sin and Death have been sitting 'idly' by the gates, but now, with the Fall as we know completed, Sin senses Satan's success:

> Methinks I feel new strength within me rise,
> Wings growing, and dominion given me large
> Beyond this deep ... (X, 243–5)

Eve, we recall, had had wings in her troubling dream (V, 87); she and Adam after their sin in eating the fruit had fancied that they felt 'Divinity within them breeding wings' (IX, 1010), and now Sin, growing confident of power, feels the same. She will go to earth, and

> Thou my shade
> Inseparable must with me along:
> For Death from Sin no power can separate. (X, 249–51)

Milton is taking up the allegory he had begun in Book II where Sin, like Eve and like Adam later, recounted her birth:

> a goddess armed
> Out of thy head I sprung (II, 757–8)

[159]

she had reminded Satan in Book II, and had described their fierce incestuous offspring Death. That satanic trinity meets again here, in Book X.

While awaiting Satan their common father, Sin and Death together build a bridge and causeway – foretold in Book II – that stretches, and will stretch until the Last Day

> Over this main from hell to that new world
> Where Satan now prevails … (X, 257–8)

'Now prevails': with bitterness, seemingly casual, Milton judges the Restoration England of his own time, the time of 'now', as an England given up to Satan; the kingdom of the saints that he had hoped for has not come about. Satan's own crossing of Chaos had been heroic and difficult; a bridge and causeway will mean that for 'all the infernal host' it will henceforth be easy. Death already 'snuffed the smell / Of mortal change on earth', and his anticipation is like that of 'a flock of ravenous fowl', vultures who come flying

> to a field,
> Where armies lie encamped … lured
> With scent of living carcasses designed
> For death, the following day, in bloody fight. (X, 275–8)

Milton's world of the Civil War battles and of Ireland was but too grimly aware of the horror behind that neat witty phrase, 'living carcasses designed / For death'. The bridge is built. Descriptions of the building of Pandæmonium and of this bridge fulfil epic's tendency to include construction-work – like that of the *Aeneid*'s Carthage. Architecture, like all the arts, gives us some consolation and flourishes in our fallen, restless and unsatisfied world. Milton's Death is a great practical builder because he has a 'mace petrific'. Smiting with this he can turn life to stone and can change the shifting matter of Chaos into fixed and stony substance, cold and dry. 'By wondrous art / Pontifical' (313–4) Sin and Death complete the bridge that will join earth to hell, and Milton, bringing out the ambiguity of 'pontifical' (its Latin root meaning 'bridge' while its primary meaning is 'episcopal'), implies satirically that Popish or other high ecclesiastical power is a direct and easy route to hell.

Satan, 'in likeness of an angel bright', is seen by Sin and Death as he flies towards them. He knew all: he had, Milton tells the reader, soon changed out of his serpent shape, and had overheard and watched as Eve tempted Adam. But when the Son came to judge he fled. Returning later, he 'gathered his own doom' as 'the hapless pair / Sat in their sad discourse' (342–3). Now, meeting his 'Fair daughter, and thou son and grandchild both', the 'prince of darkness' is 'glad', and glad that Sin and Death are so worthy of

> the race
> Of Satan (for I glory in the name,
> Antagonist of heaven's almighty king) … (X, 385–7)

He admires the bridge ('stupendous'); they part, Satan suggesting that Sin and Death make their way to Paradise,

> There dwell and reign in bliss, thence on the earth
> Dominion exercise and in the air,
> Chiefly on man, sole lord of all declared,
> Him first make sure your thrall, and lastly kill.
>   (X, 399–402)

As Sin and Death hold their course to earth, 'through thickest constellations',

> the blasted stars looked wan,
> And planets, planet-strook, real eclipse
> Then suffered. (X, 411–14)

Satan, going the other way, reaches hell, finds his chief confederates in council within Pandæmonium and, disguised as a 'plebeian angel militant / Of lowest order', reaches the 'Plutonian hall' and then, becoming

> invisible
> Ascended his high throne … (X, 444–5)

His absurd, almost endearing love of drama is close to his love of majesty, and it is as a 'shape star bright', a 'sudden blaze', that he makes the 'Stygian throng' suddenly aware of 'their mighty chief returned' (455).

Silence falls, and Satan tells of his journey to earth over the 'untractable abyss ... the womb of unoriginal Night and Chaos wild' (476–7), of the 'absolute perfection' of Paradise, and of the fraud by which man

> I have seduced
> From his creator, and the more to increase
> Your wonder, with an apple; he thereat
> Offended, worth your laughter, hath given up
> Both his beloved man and all this world,
> To Sin and Death a prey, and so to us,
> Without our hazard, labour, or alarm,
> To range in, and to dwell, and over man
> To rule ... (X, 485–93)

Satan, of course, is wrong; he is blind to the difference between his own revolt and man's disobedience. God has not given up man, but Satan believes that he, Satan, has won the battle for Adam and Eve, and boasts delightedly of his exploit. The scene of his triumph with that apple is vividly evoked as the listening thousands laugh, Satan hurrying on in his happy victorious tale; he finally dismisses as paltry and literal the judgment concerning the bruise,

> A world who would not purchase with a bruise,
> Or much more grievous pain? (X, 500–1)

'What remains, ye gods', he concludes, 'But up and enter now into full bliss' (502–3). Expecting 'universal shout and high applause' he hears

> On all sides, from innumerable tongues
> A dismal universal hiss, the sound
> Of public scorn; he wondered, but not long ... (X, 507–9)

and then he wondered at himself: he was changing,

> supplanted down he fell
> A monstrous serpent on his belly prone,
> Reluctant, but in vain, a greater power
> Now ruled him, punished in the shape he sinned …
>
> (X, 513–6)

Satan has tried to supplant God, and he finds now that his former angel form is supplanted by the monstrous creature that he really is. He can only hiss, as can his followers. They

> hiss for hiss returned with forked tongue
> To forked tongue … (X, 518–9)

All are swarming complicated monsters. Milton in this most dramatic climax has brought the aspiring rebel of the early books to recount his later action of mean fraud as though it were true heroism. In the monstrous metamorphosis Satan is both exposed for what he is and punished; the serpent and Satan, though the serpent only features in Genesis, are brilliantly recreated as one body, and questions of virtue and true heroism hover over the account.

Every epic poem is encyclopaedic of its time. Milton now draws upon his reading to list the extraordinary serpents that the fallen angels become:

> Scorpion and asp, and amphisbaena dire,
> Cerastes horned, hydrus, and ellops drear,
> And dipsas … (X, 524–6)

One would become learned indeed if one followed Milton's breadth and vastness of knowledge. The followers outside the council chamber also turn into serpents and Satan, as becomes their leader, appears larger than a huge Python, in fact a dragon; Milton must want us to remember 'the great dragon' of Revelation (12: 9), 'that old serpent, called the Devil, and Satan, which deceiveth the whole world'. Milton's Satan deceives, and is deceived along with all the other fallen angels/devils/serpents when all the snakes climb up into a grove of trees newly sprung up 'laden with fair fruit'. This has suddenly appeared by God's

[163]

will who reigns above, to aggravate
Their penance ... (X, 549–50)

God may seem to us unattractively and unremittingly punitive
to the fallen angels; we would be less so. But God is consistent
right through the poem and he acts within Milton's system of
belief: that rebellion and aspiring ambition against so just and
reasonable a ruler as God cannot be tolerated. God's punishment here is a cruel joke; in the grove, 'for one forbidden tree'
there is 'a multitude', and on all the trees, fair fruit. The serpents, 'parched with scalding thirst and hunger fierce' (556) roll
'in heaps' to the trees, climb up, but

> instead of fruit
> Chewed bitter ashes, which the offended taste
> With spattering noise rejected: oft they assayed,
> Hunger and thirst constraining ... (X, 565–8)

It is the torment of Tantalus, and Milton's fallen angels have
to undergo, 'some say', this 'humbling' annually 'to dash their
pride, and joy for man seduced' (577).

Sin and Death meanwhile arrive in Paradise. Book X moves
about, has characters meet and part, has settings in heaven, hell
and earth, has simultaneous actions, and even Milton occasion-
ally has to change narrative direction with the old-fashioned
'Meanwhile':

> Meanwhile in Paradise the hellish pair
> Too soon arrived ... (X. 585–6)

Sin comes first,

> behind her Death
> Close following pace for pace, not mounted yet
> On his pale horse ... (X, 588–90)

And I looked, and behold a pale horse: and his name
that sat on him was Death and Hell followed with him.
(Rev. 6: 8)

Right through *Paradise Lost* but more frequently in the last books Milton gives us a sense not only of the origins of things but of the endings. The death with which man is cursed in Genesis becomes the pale horse of Revelation, the book where visions and apocalypse announce the last things, the end of time. Milton's reference to the pale horse here in Book X when death has not yet hit humanity, carries with it the endless-seeming weight of time, the stretches of mortality that are to come, the distance between Genesis and Revelation. Sin is cheerful at entering upon 'our empire'; Death cares little, 'hell, or Paradise, or heaven'. He is simply hungry and all he wants is

> To stuff this maw, this vast unhide-bound corpse. (X, 601)

Sin, Death's 'incestuous mother', advises him to start on the plants, on 'herbs, fruits, and flowers / Feed first, on each beast next, and fish and fowl' (603–4). She will,

> in man residing through the race,
> His thoughts, his looks, words, actions all infect,
> And season him thy last and sweetest prey. (X, 607–9)

God has seen and heard all and he once again makes it clear to his angels that it is man's 'polluting sin' that has led to the desecration of earth by Sin and Death, who

> know not that I called and drew them thither
> My hell-hounds, to lick up the draff and filth …
> > (X, 629–30)

They will be allowed to ravage until the Last Day and the Son's final victory. Their evil is a part of the plan, God implies: Sin and Death are merely the instruments of his providence. The angels

> Sung hallelujah, as the sound of seas … (X, 642)

They praise God as just and the Son as the 'destined restorer of mankind' (646).

[165]

But nature has to be changed, creation revised, for the earth can no longer be a paradise. God's 'mighty angels' alter the sun's shining so that it

> might affect the earth with cold and heat
> Scarce tolerable ... (X, 653–4)

The planets are to have 'influence malignant'; winds will 'confound / Sea, air, and shore'; thunder 'roll with terror'; there will be 'Vapour, and mist, and exhalation hot / Corrupt and pestilent' (694–5) and

> from the north
> Of Norumbega, and the Samoed shore
> Bursting their brazen dungeon, armed with ice
> And snow and hail and stormy gust and flaw,
> Boreas, and Caecias and Argestes loud
> And Thrascias rend the woods and seas upturn.
>   (X, 695–700)

One almost expects the Jumblies to appear 'from the north / Of Norumbega, and the Samoed shore', but no one, not even Edward Lear, is so good as Milton at making proper names roll with great organ chords through long passages. And of course the places named are real places – one could look them up – and these winds are mentioned in a seventeenth-century atlas. But it is in their unfamiliar grandeur that the names insist that the climate changes are formidable, while the simple words,

> And snow and hail and stormy gust and flaw ...

make us feel that the changes are real; we have all felt these.
   Death begins to find some satisfaction:

> Beast now with beast gan war, and fowl with fowl,
> And fish with fish; to graze the herb all leaving,
> Devoured each other ... (X, 710–12)

The bears that 'gambolled' before Adam and Eve and the 'unwieldy elephant' that 'wreathed his live proboscis' 'to make

[166]

them mirth' (IV, 340ff.) live now under a new dispensation. Adam, says Milton, perhaps taking his metaphor from Hamlet's 'sea of troubles', is 'in a troubled sea of passion tossed' (718), and he remarks the change. Milton gives him a long soliloquy as, 'hid in gloomiest shade', he stays still and alone. As in Shakespeare, the soliloquy (unless it is simply to reveal matters of plot) is often a mark of unhappiness; unfallen, Adam talked, with God, with Eve, with Raphael; fallen, he examines only to himself his new complication of mental pressures and feelings. Like Satan's unhappy soliloquies, Adam's is an inner debate. His 'highth of happiness', he says, had been to behold the face of God. The loss is 'misery, I deserved it, and would bear my own deservings', but the injunction 'Increase and multiply' will bring upon him the 'execration' 'of all ages to succeed'; the curses shall

> with a fierce reflux on me redound,
> On me as on their natural centre light
> Heavy ... (X, 739–41)

Milton clearly enjoys the, perhaps confusing, juxtaposition of 'light' ('alight') and 'Heavy', stressed at the beginning of the next line; so heavy indeed will be the execration that Adam breaks out before the line ends,

> O fleeting joys
> Of Paradise, dear bought with lasting woes! (X, 741–2)

His exclamation is the story of the poem: 'fleeting' and 'lasting', 'joys' and 'woes' with a wealth of meaning in 'dear'. Adam would prefer not to be:

> Did I request thee, Maker, from my clay
> To mould me man, did I solicit thee ... (X, 743–4)

Failure oppresses Adam. The prohibition, when he first spoke of it to Eve in the garden, was 'this one, this easy charge' (IV, 421); now, he admits as he mentally addresses God that he was 'unable to perform / Thy terms too hard' (750–1). Furthermore,

> why hast thou added
> The sense of endless woes? Inexplicable
> Thy justice seems ... (X, 753–5)

There is an aggrieved accusing note here; it does not last. Adam reasonably recollects that he had accepted God's terms:

> wilt thou enjoy the good,
> Then cavil the conditions? (X, 758–9)

He asks himself,

> what if thy son
> Prove disobedient, and reproved, retort,
> Wherefore didst thou beget me? I sought it not: (X, 760–2)

The question has been asked many times since, and it is a measure of Adam's maturing into a complex human being like us all, that he can imagine a future, and that that future might have resemblances to his own experience. He is beginning to live in time and to accumulate a history. He sees, too, that unlike his own sons, who will be born through 'natural necessity', he has an absolute commitment to the Father, for God made him 'of choice his own'. 'Thy punishment then justly is at his will', he tells himself, and submits, 'his doom is fair' (763–70). He badly wants that punishment, death:

> How gladly would I meet
> Mortality my sentence, and be earth
> Insensible, how glad would lay me down
> As in my mother's lap? (X, 775–8)

He knew no mother but the earth, the clay of his being: the phrase, 'as in my mother's lap' that Milton uses to express a death wish is a common phrase, universally recognised, for Adam is Everyman; his guilt and despair echo down the centuries. In death, continues Adam,

> I should rest
> And sleep secure; his dreadful voice no more
> Would thunder in my ears ... (X, 778–80)

Adam's natural and theologically naïve view that death is un-troubled sleep – Hamlet knew better – is equalled by the size of his guilt: God's voice had in fact been mild when pronouncing judgment, but in Adam's imagination it is like thunder. He has one great fear – that he will not be able totally to die, that

> the spirit of man
> Which God inspired, cannot together perish
> With this corporeal clod ... (X, 784–6)

Does the spirit die with the body? Why should the body die and not the spirit? It was the spirit that sinned; is God's 'wrath without end?' In the grave will he, Adam, suffer a living death, endless? Adam puts many questions to himself, and can find no answers. Milton himself apparently held the somewhat hereti-cal view that the whole of man, spirit and body, dies at death, and then, at the Day of Judgment, the whole of man is restored to life. Adam, beyond his worry about the meaning of death for himself, is tormented about his legacy:

> Ah, why should all mankind
> For one man's fault thus guiltless be condemned,
> If guiltless? (X, 822–4)

He has asked a huge, vexed question about original sin, and he answers it in theologically accepted fashion himself:

> But from me what can proceed,
> But all corrupt, both mind and will depraved ... (X, 824–5)

His posterity will inevitably 'will the same / With me'. He again absolves God of injustice:

> all my evasions vain,
> And reasonings, though through mazes, lead me still
> But to my own conviction: first and last
> On me, me only, as the source and spring
> Of all corruption, all the blame lights due ... (X, 829–33)

The 'mazes' of his reasonings remind the reader of the fallen angels who had lost the truth, but who yet

[169]

> reasoned high
> Of providence, foreknowledge, will and fate,
> Fixed fate, free will, foreknowledge absolute,
> And found no end, in wandering mazes lost. (II, 558–61)

Adam is not in such darkness as were the fallen angels; the mazes of his reasoning have led him to the firm conviction of guilt and the justness of punishment. This is the first stage on the way to repentance. Confession, to the self in the first instance, is a beginning. Adam has still some way to go on his spiritual journey; it is one that Milton as a Christian and a Puritan took seriously. Instead of moving towards contrition, however, Adam is in danger of falling into the trap of bitterness – he speaks glancingly of Eve as 'that bad woman' – and into despair, likening himself to Satan 'in crime and doom':

> O conscience! into what abyss of fears
> And horrors hast thou driven me; out of which
> I find no way, from deep to deeper plunged! (X, 842–4)

His 'umpire conscience' which God placed within man as a guide (III, 194–5), has not been listened to, and Adam has within him an 'abyss of fears', the psychological equivalent of Satan's 'wild abyss' on the brink of hell, where Chaos was umpire, not conscience. For Adam,

> on the ground
> Outstretched he lay, on the cold ground, and oft
> Cursed his creation ...
> Why comes not death ... (X, 850–4)

His long soliloquy ends with an elegiac lament that recalls his former happiness, his ecstatic morning celebration with Eve in praise of God's creation, of 'hill or valley, fountain, or fresh shade' (V, 203). All is now different:

> O woods, O fountains, hillocks, dales and bowers,
> With other echo late I taught your shades
> To answer, and resound far other song. (X, 860–2)

[170]

'Sad Eve beheld, / Desolate where she sat'; she approaches and is angrily repulsed,

> Out of my sight, thou serpent … (X, 867)

Adam launches into a tirade of recrimination and anti-feminist abuse; he castigates Eve's 'wandering vanity', says that

> all was but a show
> Rather than solid virtue, all but a rib
> Crooked by nature, bent, as now appears,
> More to the part sinister … (X, 883–6)

wonders why earth was not more like heaven, filled with 'spirits masculine' only, why God had not found

> some other way to generate
> Mankind … (X, 894–5)

and foresees

> innumerable
> Disturbances on earth through female snares …
> (X, 896–7)

Man 'never shall find out fit mate', concludes Adam, as he bitterly lists the misfortunes, mistakes, parental and perverse obstacles that will so often lead to marriage with the wrong woman,

> Which infinite calamity shall cause
> To human life, and household peace confound.
> (X, 907–8)

Milton allows (perhaps in one part of himself even encourages) Adam in his anger and despair to voice the distorted views of generally received misogyny. Eve endures it all, and makes no defence against his attack. He turns away,

> but Eve
> Not so repulsed, with tears that ceased not flowing,
> And tresses all disordered, at his feet

[171]

> Fell humble, and embracing them, besought
> His peace ... (X, 909–13)

Milton is describing an icon. Eve is the first St Mary Magdalene, the penitent woman at the feet of man, described in Luke (7: 38), painted by Titian and a favourite of later artists. Eve's abasement and supplication seem less a device to mollify the patriarchal ego than genuine repentance, love and need. Her language has a steadiness and balance quite unlike Adam's angry ranting:

> Forsake me not thus, Adam ...
> ... bereave me not,
> Whereon I live, thy gentle looks, thy aid,
> Thy counsel in this uttermost distress,
> My only strength and stay: forlorn of thee,
> Whither shall I betake me ... (X, 914–22)

Vulnerable, she now accepts blame; previously she had blamed Adam; this is proper, though there is something excessive in Eve's wish to take on all the punishment:

> ... that all
> The sentence from thy head removed may light
> On me, sole cause to thee of all this woe,
> Me me only just object of his ire. (X, 933–6)

The insistent desire to take on all the retribution – 'on me' – recalls the Son's pleading with the Father:

> Behold me then, me for him, life for life
> I offer, on me let thine anger fall;
> Account me man ... (III, 236–8)

The Son's sacrifice will be the ultimate redeeming act, but we have perhaps to see Eve here as a humble instrument of grace, one who initiates the way to forgiveness: she breaks the cycle of anger and despair. In Adam she

> wrought
> Commiseration; soon his heart relented

> Towards her, his life so late and sole delight,
> Now at his feet submissive in distress … (X, 939–42)

Because he can feel compassion for Eve he can perhaps begin to envisage compassion from God. Like Eve, he now more than acknowledges his own fault and, in his manly seventeenth-century way, he resolves to pray

> That on my head all might be visited,
> Thy frailty and infirmer sex forgiven,
> To me committed and by me exposed. (X, 955–7)

Sensibly, like man and wife, they move on from this competition about who is the more to blame, and Adam suggests that they

> strive
> In offices of love, how we may lighten
> Each other's burden in our share of woe; (X, 959–61)

This is an active sharing, not a blaming; Adam will leave anger and vengeful thoughts behind and seek new ways to love. This is so different from Satan's attitude to his fall: his thoughts were of revenge, and of the desire to repeat upon others the harm done to him. Adam has a capacity to begin afresh, a capacity not to repeat. But the recovery from such a trauma as they have had is not achieved in an easy straight line; there are haltings and windings by the way, since Milton has Adam and Eve work out their possibility of salvation through discussion and within their limited human knowledge.

Adam realises, as Eve as has not, that death is not going to be sudden; it will come as

> a slow-paced evil,
> A long day's dying to augment our pain,
> And to our seed (O hapless seed!) derived. (X, 963–5)

The hapless seed could be spared the misery of death, thinks Eve, if, simply, they were not born:

> Childless thou art, childless remain:
> So death shall be deceived his glut, and with us two
> Be forced to satisfy his ravenous maw. (X, 989–91)

And if it prove too difficult to 'abstain / From love's due rites, nuptial embraces sweet' while both are 'languishing' with desire,

> Let us seek death, or he not found, supply
> With our own hands his office on our selves; (X, 1001–2)

Eve's cheek turns pale as she makes these two shocking suggestions, childlessness and suicide; the first would seem wicked in an age when people had many children in the hope that one or two would survive; and the second was a sin in any Christian thinking: Spenser had included a powerful advocacy for suicide in his *Faerie Queene*, but he had given it to his allegorical character Despair. Adam is 'nothing swayed' by Eve's counsel and his mind moves to 'better hopes', as, having to reply to Eve, he finds himself discovering in himself thoughts that will bring him, and Eve, to total co-operation with God. He realises that God will not be forestalled and that a death 'snatched', as Eve suggests,

> will not exempt us from the pain
> We are by doom to pay ... (X, 1025–6)

He looks for a new way out, and calls to mind the sentence 'that thy seed shall bruise / The serpent's head' (1031–2); he conjectures that the serpent was 'our grand foe Satan', and that their own childless death would defeat God's purpose here. He bids Eve remember, as he now remembers himself,

> with what mild
> And gracious temper he both heard and judged
> Without wrath or reviling ... (X, 1046–8)

He reminds her that death had not come immediately but that, for Eve,

> Pains only in child-bearing were foretold ... (X, 1051)

and for himself that

> with labour I must earn
> My bread; what harm? Idleness had been worse;
> (X, 1054–5)

He reminds her that the Son had

> Clothed us unworthy, pitying while he judged; (X, 1059)

Entirely convinced of God's justice, Adam is now beginning to discover signs of God's mercy; he is clearly, of his own free will, going to involve himself in human history that is a part of a divine ordering. The Son, he believes, will show them more than how to clothe themselves,

> How much more, if we pray him, will his ear
> Be open ... (X, 1060–1)

'He will instruct us praying', says Adam; yet, fallen man as he now is in a fallen world, he has to use his inventiveness and his intelligence. Already, as he speaks to Eve,

> the winds
> Blow moist and keen, shattering the graceful locks
> Of these fair spreading trees ... (X, 1065–7)

and Adam has thought of ideas about how to make fire to keep them warm: two ideas: one, by concentrating beams of light upon 'matter sere', the other, by 'collision of two bodies' – presumably friction. Technology begins. Altogether Adam is challenged and stimulated by the fallen condition and has no fear that they will not

> pass commodiously this life, sustained
> By him with many comforts, till we end
> In dust, our final rest and native home. (X, 1083–5)

Finally, Adam suggests that they seal their new commitment to God:

> What better can we do, than to the place
> Repairing where he judged us, prostrate fall

[175]

Before him reverent, and there confess
Humbly our faults, and pardon beg, with tears
Watering the ground, and with our sighs the air
Frequenting, sent from hearts contrite, in sign
Of sorrow unfeigned, and humiliation meek. (X, 1086–92)

'Undoubtedly', continues Adam, 'he will relent and turn /
From his displeasure', for when he had seemed most angry
and severe,

What else but favour, grace, and mercy shone?
    So spake our father penitent, nor Eve
Felt less remorse … (X, 1096–8)

Milton has taken the reader carefully through the stages of
Adam's shame, misery, anger, contempt, self-pity, conviction of
guilt, conviction of justice, sympathy, energy, hope and finally
the realisation of God's mercy,

What else but favour, grace, and mercy shone?

The words take us back to God's promise in Book III, speaking
of his mercy and justice, that 'mercy first and last shall brightest
shine' (III, 134). Adam can now properly be called 'penitent',
and Milton uses that word. Book X ends as Adam and Eve do
what Adam suggested: they make their joint confession and
perform their act of contrition. Milton invests their action with
a formal dignity by having the reader go through it twice, once
in Adam's suggestion, quoted above, and a second time in narrative form, so that we move outside Adam and Eve, and are, as it
were, witnesses to an act of devotion:

they forthwith to the place
Repairing where he judged them prostrate fell
Before him reverent, and both confessed
Humbly their faults, and pardon begged, with tears
Watering the ground, and with their sighs the air
Frequenting, sent from hearts contrite, in sign
Of sorrow unfeigned, and humiliation meek.
                                             (X, 1098–1104)

Book X has seen Adam and Eve begin their education and development into plain ordinary man and wife, and it has seen two bridges built, one joining hell to earth and the other re-joining man to heaven by reconciliation and repentance.

BOOK XI

BOOKS XI AND XII continue the education of Adam and Eve. Milton cannot have them venturing into the world outside Paradise in any way less equipped than the readers of *Paradise Lost*. Milton's readers are themselves fallen human beings like Adam and Eve, but they have the advantage over our first parents of knowing history, and, better informed, they can approach with more discrimination the moral choices that knowledge of good and evil has brought. Milton, of course, says nothing of this. He shows Adam history, history for us, the future for him, particularly the history of man's relations with God. Adam's changing reactions measure his developing ability to judge correctly.

The prayers and contrition of Adam and Eve are noticed in heaven and the Son points out to the Father that this offering is of more worth than anything Adam's 'own hand manuring all the trees / Of Paradise could have produced, ere fallen / From innocence' (28–30). History for Adam will be an escalating plunge into catastrophe, 'all our woe' (I, 3) since the Fall; at the same time, as a kind of counter-point to this, man will have the chance to develop a richer spiritual and inner life because fallen; the Son already discerns the beginning of this in Adam.

God has had it all in mind. After a life 'tried in sharp tribulation, and refined / By faith and faithful works' man will have 'second life' (63–4). The great trumpets sound in heaven, 'perhaps once more / To sound at general doom', the angels take their seats. God explains what has happened and requests Michael, the greatest of the archangels,

> Haste thee, and from the Paradise of God
> Without remorse drive out the sinful pair … (XI, 104–5)

But they are not to go out ignorant,

> reveal
> To Adam what shall come in future days … (XI, 113–4)

Adam, meanwhile, still in Paradise, knowing what repentance
means, is beginning to discover that further component of religious commitment – faith. He feels that 'prayer, / Or one short
sigh of human breath' can in fact be 'upborne / Even to the
seat of God' (146–8). For themselves, he is hopeful that

> the bitterness of death
> Is past, and we shall live. Whence hail to thee,
> Eve rightly called, Mother of all Mankind,
> Mother of all things living … (XI, 157–60)

His words anticipate the salutation to Mary, 'Hail Mary', and
they thus ensure that the comfort of the Redemption is in the
reader's mind before Adam's education into the nightmare of
history begins. There is a new optimism in Adam's words, and
in Eve's reply; she will work at Adam's side, 'never … henceforth to stray',

> till day droop; while here we dwell,
> What can be toilsome in these pleasant walks?
> Here let us live, though in fallen state, content. (XI, 178–80)

The precarious contentment is dashed at once as an eagle,

> The bird of Jove, stooped from his airy tower,
> Two birds of gayest plume before him drove …

At the same time, a lion,

> the beast that reigns in woods,
> First hunter then, pursued a gentle brace,
> Goodliest of all the forest, hart and hind … (XI, 185–9)

'Adam observed' these acts, and was 'not unmoved'. He recognised that nature was giving signs of the state of things to
come. 'After tea', wrote Dorothy Wordsworth in her Journal
in Grasmere on 2 February 1802, 'I read aloud the 11th Book

of Paradise Lost we were much impressed & also melted into tears.' There is much to grieve for in Book XI, and this vignette of aggression in nature must have contributed to the Wordsworths' sense of grief. Milton describes Adam's feeling in the negative form: he was 'not unmoved', a phrase that alone would have attracted Wordsworth, himself a subtle user of negatives. Dorothy's Journal is helpful. Another entry, weeks later, for 17 April 1802, points closely to this particular passage in Book XI as a source of the Wordsworths' emotion: 'I saw a Robin chacing a scarlet Butterfly this morning.' Next day, 18 April 1802, Dorothy wrote, 'we sate in the orchard – William wrote the poem on the Robin & the Butterfly.' Milton's eagle pursues two beautiful birds, his lion is hunting deer, Dorothy's Robin chases a scarlet Butterfly: Wordsworth, like Adam, was 'not unmoved'. He wrote (not himself too impressively):

> Could Father Adam open his eyes
> And see this sight beneath the skies,
> He'd wish to close them again.
> ('The Redbreast Chasing the Butterfly', 12–14)

Father Adam in *Paradise Lost* might have wished to but could not close his eyes; he realised that these signs of aggression in nature were ominous.

The Archangel Michael, laying aside his glory and 'as man / Clad to meet man' (239–40), approached. At Adam's request Eve dutifully retired, but she over-heard Michael:

> to remove thee I am come,
> And send thee from the garden forth to till
> The ground whence thou wast taken, fitter soil. (XI, 260–2)

at which she emerged immediately in distress:

> O flowers,
> That never will in other climate grow,
> My early visitation, and my last
> At even, which I bred up with tender hand
> From the first opening bud, and gave ye names,
> Who now shall rear ye to the sun ... (XI, 273–8)

She had named the flowers as Adam had named the creatures and it is as though they are her children. She is a woman leaving her home:

> Thee lastly nuptial bower …
>   … from thee
> How shall I part, and whither wander down
> Into a lower world, to this obscure
> And wild, how shall we breathe in other air
> Less pure, accustomed to immortal fruits? (XI, 280–5)

The phrase 'immortal fruits' might have had an unfortunate resonance and the angel 'interrupted mild',

> Lament not Eve, but patiently resign
> What justly thou hast lost … (XI, 287–8)

'Patiently resign': patience will be a new virtue for Eve to learn; she has never needed this essential of the spiritual life; even so disciplined a Christian as Hopkins found it hard:

> Patience, hard thing! The hard thing but to pray,
> But bid for, Patience is!

Michael goes on to suggest to Eve that she is being 'over-fond' of place: she will not after all be lonely; she will be with her husband,

> Where he abides, think there thy native soil. (XI, 292)

These things are in the mind.

Adam, 'heart-strook' at the news that they must leave the garden, speaks his grief, not for domestic loss, but that he will no longer be near the places where he has had contact with God:

>   here I could frequent,
> With worship, place by place where he vouchsafed
> Presence divine, and to my sons relate;
> On this mount he appeared; under this tree
>   … among these pines
>   … at this fountain … (XI, 317–22)

[182]

In Milton's view it was a failing (and perhaps particularly a Catholic failing) to need places with associations, either to encourage memory or to stimulate devotion. 'In yonder nether world', bemoans Adam,

> where shall I seek
> His bright appearances, or footstep trace? (XI, 328–9)

Michael makes it clear that everything is God's – heaven, 'all the earth. / Not this rock only' (335–6). It is Paradise, the beautiful garden, that is thus slightingly identified as 'this rock', and the implication is that no place has a special investment in God; not even, by a further implication, the celebrated 'rock' of St Peter in Rome. Signs of God may be found any and everywhere, and 'of his steps the track divine' (354). It is Adam's task now, as Michael shows him scenes from what to us is history and what to him is vision, to find and trace 'the track divine' and to 'learn / True patience'.

Eve sleeps, for Michael has 'drenched her eyes'; she will not waken until towards the end of Book XII.

> On a huge hill,
> Cragged, and steep, Truth stands,

John Donne had written firmly in the early part of the century, and like Donne in his imagination, and like many others taking spiritual journeys to Truth, Michael and Adam climb to the top of a high hill, and the lessons begin. Milton here, and for the rest of Book XI, is writing in the tradition of vision-literature; saints and writers from the Book of Revelation through Chaucer, the Middle Ages and beyond, have written about religious truth in terms of vision. We may be less familiar with that visionary convention than were Milton's first readers – who would be reading *Pilgrim's Progress* within a few years – but we can respond with Adam to the brief narratives and can appreciate Milton's structural design.

The first thing Adam sees is a sweeping vision of the great civilisations and kingdoms of the earth; proper names of places from Cambalu and Samarchand to Ophir, Almansor and Rome, make the verse thick and magical with an exotic geography and history. Michael is giving Adam an overwhelming lesson in the length of time that is to come, the varieties of human society that will develop, and the rise and decline of empires. His vision demonstrates more emphatically perhaps than words (Milton uses words to present visions!) how long, how despairingly long, mankind will have to wait before the Last Day and the Second Coming. Patience is indeed to be a paramount Christian virtue. Yet there are bridges across these vast stretches of time; Milton, like most readers of the Bible, links Eve to Mary, Adam to Christ, the vision from the high hill here to that quite other hill where 'the tempter set / Our second Adam in the wilderness, / To show him all earth's kingdoms and their glory' (382–4). The Son, 'Our second Adam' (383) will not be touched by this display of earthly grandeur; the first Adam, looking from his hill, must be at once cheered by man's achievements and desolated by the long wait that has to stretch through history. He is swept through the epic panorama of human societies, and then Michael has him turn to contrasting scenes of detail. Milton clearly accepts the Renaissance concept of history – that its function is to instruct; after the general picture, Michael focuses upon specific and significant episodes. First, he has to prepare Adam: with herbs – euphrasy (eyebright) and rue – he cleanses Adam's eyes from the film that the forbidden fruit had caused, and three drops from the well of life help Adam, 'Even to the inmost seat of mental sight' (418), to see the significance of action and to interpret.

The first scene is of two men sacrificing at an altar, one offering fruits and corn, the second 'the firstlings of his flock'. This latter sacrifice seems propitious, and the first man, envious, violently kills the second. Adam's first lesson is one of terrible human conflict and the sight of a pious man unjustly, brutally killed.

> Is piety thus and pure devotion paid? (XI, 452)

His horror increases when he learns that the two men, unnamed by Michael, are his own sons; they are Cain and Abel, and in their story Adam sees death for the first time and is shocked at the violence. He had been 'not unmoved' by fallen nature's aggression in that first sky pursuit and forest chase; at the aggression of fallen man the pain is multiplied. Michael assures him that there are other and 'many shapes of death': violence, a result of envy and anger he has now seen; disease, the result of intemperance, will make abundantly clear

> What misery the inabstinence of Eve
> Shall bring on men. (XI, 476–7)

With this comprehensive condemnation Michael shows Adam a lazar-house and Milton presents in a compendium of seventeenth-century medical terms the deformed and diseased of humanity crowded within. Adam wept,

> Though not of woman born; compassion quelled
> His best of man, and gave him up to tears … (XI, 495–7)

His response, the wrong response, is that it would be better not to be born. He cannot understand why the image of God in man should be so debased and deformed (500–14). Michael answers, always a moralist, that 'ungoverned appetite … Inductive mainly to the sin of Eve' (516–19) and the failure to reverence God's image in themselves is the basic cause of the diseased body.

> I yield it just, said Adam, and submit. (XI, 526)

Yet he asks if there is another way to come at death, and Michael, like a didactic poet of an earlier era, advocates

> The rule of not too much, by temperance taught …
> So mayst thou live, till like ripe fruit thou drop
> Into thy mother's lap, or be with ease
> Gathered, not harshly plucked, for death mature …
>   (XI, 531–7)

The corollary of an easy death is old age, and Michael's picture of this is the accepted 'Sans teeth, sans eyes, sans taste, sans everything' of Jaques in *As You Like It*. It makes Adam feel that he would not 'prolong / Life much, bent rather how I may be quit / Fairest and easiest of this cumbrous charge' (547–9), only to be told by Michael that he must try for a more objective stance:

> Nor love thy life, nor hate; but what thou livest
> Live well, how long or short permit to heaven ...
>
> (XI, 553–4)

The next scene presented to Adam is drawn more directly from Genesis (chapters 4 and 6), and it pleases him. Amid tents upon a spacious plain and cattle grazing is heard the 'melodious chime' of harp and organ, and not far off is a forge where one stood 'labouring', inventive in things that can be wrought from brass and iron. Men from the mountains come down, and they too seem pious and just men, 'all their study bent / To worship God aright and know his works' (577–8) and, beyond that, to give their minds to 'those things ... which might preserve / Freedom and peace to men' (579–80), things, we perceive, like music and the creative and applied arts. But from the tents come

> A bevy of fair women, richly gay
> In gems and wanton dress; to the harp they sung
> Soft amorous ditties, and in dance came on; (XI, 582–4)

Quite clearly, in the 'wanton dress', in their appeal to the eye, their lack of reasonable converse, this must be fallen eroticism.

> The men though grave, eyed them, and let their eyes
> Rove without rein, till in the amorous net
> Fast caught ...
>   in heat
> They light the nuptial torch ...
> With feast and music all the tents resound. (XI, 585–92)

Marriages are made without due seriousness, but, after the diseases and deformities of old age, it seems good to have here

> love and youth not lost, songs, garlands, flowers ...
>
> (XI, 594)

Adam is delighted:

> Here nature seems fulfilled in all her ends. (XI, 602)

He is wrong again. Michael is clear:

> Judge not what is best
> By pleasure … (XI, 603–4)

Fulfilling nature is not enough; there is a

> nobler end
> Holy and pure, conformity divine. (XI, 605–6)

The pleasant tents are the dwellings of the descendants of Cain, while the men 'studious … / Of arts that polish life, inventors rare' (the sons of Seth) are

> Unmindful of their maker, though his Spirit
> Taught them, but they his gifts acknowledged none.
> (XI, 611–12)

Their beautiful offspring are

> Bred only …
> to sing, to dance,
> To dress, and troll the tongue, and roll the eye.
> (XI, 618–20)

And to them the

> sober race of men, whose lives
> Religious titled them the sons of God,
> Shall yield up all their virtue … (XI, 621–3)

They all now 'swim in joy / (Erelong to swim at large)' (625–6); Milton in this dark joke points to the Flood, and Adam, 'of short joy bereft', has to revise his opinion and move to pity for those who turned aside from the right way; 'but still', he concludes,

> I see the tenor of man's woe
> Holds on the same, from woman to begin. (XI, 632–3)

[187]

Again, he has to be corrected; Michael gives short shrift to Adam's misogyny:

> From man's effeminate slackness it begins,
>   Said the angel ... (XI, 634–5)

There are two more visionary scenes in Book XI. Each of these expands to greater and more terrible effect themes already set in motion: aggression, irreligion and self-indulgence. The first scene is of cities with 'lofty gates and towers', and men with 'fierce faces threatening war', foaming steeds, 'fair oxen and fair kine' driven as booty over the plain, while the 'ensanguined field'

> Where cattle pastured late, now scattered lies
>   With carcasses and arms ... (XI, 653–4)

and is deserted. There is as well a siege of a city,

>   by battery, scale and mine,
>   Assaulting; others from the wall defend
>   With dart and javelin, stones and sulphurous fire;
>   On each hand slaughter and gigantic deeds. (XI, 656–9)

There is a meeting of 'gray-headed men and grave, with warriors mixed' (662), and these are soon

> In factious opposition, till at last
>   Of middle age one rising, eminent
>   In wise deport, spake much of right and wrong,
>   Of justice, of religion, truth, and peace,
>   And judgment from above: him old and young
>   Exploded and had seized with violent hands,
>   Had not a cloud descending snatched him thence
>   Unseen amid the throng ... (XI, 664–71)

Adam is seeing war: 'violence / ... and oppression, and sword-law / Through all the plain, and refuge none was found (671–3). He can now encompass great numbers of men killing and men slain, and has come a long way, one might say, from the eagle and the lion pursuing smaller creatures. The one man

in the war-scene who spoke of right and wrong was shouted
down ('exploded') and caused little interruption. The violence
proceeded.

> Adam was all in tears, and to his guide
> Lamenting turned full sad; O what are these,
> Death's ministers, not men, who thus deal death
> Inhumanly to men, and multiply
> Ten thousand fold the sin of him who slew
> His brother ... (XI, 674–9)

'But who was that just man'? he asks Michael. Milton, as
Michael answers, spends some time in attacking the rule of
might:

> To overcome in battle, and subdue
> Nations, and bring home spoils with infinite
> Manslaughter, shall be held the highest pitch
> Of human glory, and for glory done
> Of triumph, to be styled great conquerors,
> Patrons of mankind, gods, and sons of gods,
> Destroyers rightlier called and plagues of men. (XI, 691–7)

Whenever possible Milton attacks the rule of might; his tableau
here shows that many men love it. *Paradise Lost* is an attempt
to wean men from their liking for aggression; the cities busy
destroying themselves and each other here might be the Cities
of the Plain, might well be Sodom and Gomorrah. They are
not named, for they might be any cities, any countries at any
time. The one just man whom Adam asks about might well be
Enoch, but is of course also any man who dares to be

> The only righteous in a world perverse,
> And therefore hated, therefore so beset
> With foes for daring single to be just,
> And utter odious truth, that God would come
> To judge them with his saints ... (XI, 701–5)

He is Abdiel too (VI, 896–903); he is Milton who had himself
an urge to intervene in human history – as poet, for example,

to warn Adam and Eve to avoid their fate, and as himself to write a *Ready and Easy Way to establish a Free Commonwealth* in 1659, bringing out a second edition as late as 1660, on the very eve of Restoration. Enoch, the single just man here, is saved by God's cloud descending; but not many just men can rely on miracle; Wordsworth as a boy, not heroic but simply unable to believe that he would ever die, 'used to brood over the stories of Enoch and Elijah, & almost to persuade myself that … I should be translated in something of the same way to heaven.' (*Fenwick Notes of William Wordsworth*, ed. Jared Curtis, London, 1993, 61.) Such a 'translation' as came to Enoch was glorious recognition certainly, but it did nothing to regenerate society; how can the single activist alter the tragic shape of history?

Just as Cain's individual murder has escalated to war in the visions selected by Michael for Adam's education, so does the 'bevy of fair women' from the tents become a whole world

> turned to jollity and game,
> To luxury and riot, feast and dance,
> Marrying or prostituting, as befell,
> Rape or adultery, where passing fair
> Allured them; thence from cups to civil broils. (XI, 714–8)

Again, 'a reverend sire' preached

> Conversion and repentance, as to souls
> In prison under judgments imminent:
> But all in vain … (XI, 724–6)

This just man is not taken up by a cloud nor has he a sympathetic society to run to as the champion Abdiel had when he left Satan's rebelling angels and went back to heaven; this man is isolated. He

> removed his tents far off;
> Then from the mountain hewing timber tall,
> Began to build a vessel of huge bulk … (XI, 727–9)

As in Genesis (chapters 6 and 7) – though insects, unless included in 'creeping things', are not mentioned in the Bible –

> every beast, and bird, and insect small
> Came sevens, and pairs, and entered in ... (XI, 734–5)

God's judgment for world-scale corruption is to drown the world and begin again; his drastic action will be re-told in Ovid's myth (*Metamorphoses*, I and *Paradise Lost*, XI, 11–14) about Deucalion, also surviving a universal flood and replacing bad men by better men in a better world. Milton draws effectively upon Ovid: sea-creatures found in unlikely places (upon mountains in Ovid) and the account of the rain falling 'till the earth / No more was seen' (744–5) would remind Milton's readers of the Latin poet and thus add the force of myth to the fierce power of biblical history. Milton's ark floats, as

> sea covered sea,
> Sea without shore; and in their palaces
> Where luxury late reigned, sea monsters whelped
> And stabled ... (XI, 749–52)

The splendours of Pandaemonium and the luxuries of the palaces of both Laudian England and the Restoration doubtless deserved no less in Milton's view, and his iconoclastic bent seems much in sympathy with God's judgment.

But, comments the poet,

> How didst thou grieve then, Adam, to behold,
> The end of all thy offspring, end so sad,
> Depopulation; thee another flood,
> Of tears and sorrow a flood thee also drowned,
> And sunk thee as thy sons. (XI, 754–8)

It is terrible to Adam to have this knowledge of the future – descendants that

> torment me ere their being,
> With thought that they must be. Let no man seek
> Henceforth to be foretold what shall befall
> Him or his children, evil he may be sure ... (XI, 769–72)

He fears total destruction for the ark's cargo and is close to despair:

[191]

>   I had hope
> When violence was ceased, and war on earth,
> All would have then gone well, peace would have crowned
> With length of happy days the race of man;
> But I was far deceived; for now I see
> Peace to corrupt no less than war to waste. (XI, 779–84)

Adam is learning to analyse history and Michael seems to agree with what he concludes about peace and war, and indeed confirms the analysis: that wars, though they demonstrate 'prowess eminent and great exploits' are 'of true virtue void' (789–90), and when they have 'spilt much blood, and done much waste / Subduing nations' (791–2) the victors

>   change their course to pleasure, ease, and sloth,
> Surfeit, and lust, till wantonness and pride
> Raise out of friendship hostile deeds in peace. (XI, 794–6)

Wars begin again. This is a cyclical view of history: aggression alternates with long periods of national dissipation.

However, Michael's good news to Adam is that the one just man will remain alive. Apart from him and his company in the ark, God in judgment will destroy everything living upon earth. Perhaps the force of God's destructive power is most felt by the reader through Milton's emphasis on the destruction of Paradise; 'this mount / Of Paradise', the very place where Adam and Michael are speaking will be

>   pushed by the horned flood,
> With all his verdure spoiled, and trees adrift
> Down the great river to the opening gulf,
> And there take root an island salt and bare,
> The haunt of seals and orcs, and sea-mews' clang. (XI, 831–5)

Adam does not lament this; he has learnt

>   that God attributes to place
> No sanctity, if none be thither brought
> By men who there frequent … (XI, 836–7)

The reader sees that Milton's beliefs are strong enough for him to destroy what he himself as a poet has imaginatively created, that ideal place, Paradise. The Protestant in Spenser had had to tear down the Bower of Bliss (*Faerie Queene*, II, xii, stanza 83), and the Puritan in Milton has to wash away the paradise garden and turn it into 'an island salt and bare', ending up somewhere possibly in the Persian Gulf. This is an extreme and dramatic image for the punishment of sinfulness, and the vulnerability of whatever is created is harshly stressed; *Paradise Lost* itself, Milton's own great creation, could suffer equally. We are reminded that history is littered with terrifying iconoclastic moments. In the service of God Milton applauds this one and Adam wastes no time on it.

He watches as the north wind

> blowing dry
> Wrinkled the face of deluge, as decayed;
> And the clear sun on his wide watery glass
> Gazed hot, and of the fresh wave largely drew,
> As after thirst ... (XI, 842–6)

The waters are receding, and as we know from Genesis, on the dove's second time of flying out of the ark to spy

> Green tree or ground whereon his foot may light ...
> (XI, 858)

the bird returns with an olive leaf. A rainbow appears, and Adam rejoices,

> Far less I now lament for one whole world
> Of wicked sons destroyed, than I rejoice
> For one man found so perfect and so just,
> That God vouchsafes to raise another world ...
> (XI, 874–7)

So good a pupil has he become under the archangel's guidance that even as he asks the question he reaches the answer himself as to the meaning of the rainbow:

[193]

> But say, what mean those coloured streaks in heaven,
> Distended as the brow of God appeased … (XI, 879–80)

God is appeased and Michael explains the Covenant: that God 'relents, not to blot out mankind, / And makes a Covenant never to destroy / The earth again by flood' (891–3). The rainbow will remind man of this promise. The earth will go on until the Judgment Day in its seasons. Milton adapts the last verse of Genesis (8: 22): 'While the earth remaineth, seed-time and harvest, and cold and heat, and summer and winter, and day and night shall not cease.' This familiar cycle is near the heart of the real comfort of the fallen world and of this poem; Adam will no longer labour to find order and meaning in the world; Michael will no longer show him visions. It is enough that Book XI ends with Adam's knowledge that grace will reward the good spiritual life, that he will continue to live in a fallen world, but one with great natural comfort, and that throughout it all God is working through history towards a definite end:

> day and night,
> Seed time and harvest, heat and hoary frost
> Shall hold their course, till fire purge all things new,
> Both heaven and earth, wherein the just shall dwell.
> (XI, 898–901)

'We were much impressed & also melted into tears', Dorothy Wordsworth had written when she had finished reading aloud Book XI in 1802. Was it aggression in nature and the relentless drive to war and hedonism in man that made the Wordsworths weep? Was it Adam's gradual acceptance that that indeed was the condition of society, and that the single individual here and there must keep alive faith within himself of God's ultimate purpose, that much impressed them? Was it Milton's controlled handling of structure, the themes expanding and deepening until both Adam and the reader are able to accept the book's climax, the destruction of Paradise as an external place? Was it the quiet coda of the receding waters and the certain recurrence of the changing seasons? Was it the ability to make the Bible stories resonate for this poem's purpose? Or the ability to write in the plain style befitting a fallen world, with not an epic simile in sight; to move daringly away from the high rhetoric of Satan's language or the rich associations of allusion? Was it that Milton chose the hard spiritual path in these last books, that he made the action an inner action? Adam does not act; he responds, feels and thinks. The action has moved to action within the mind. There is not the lively immediacy of earlier books, but there is perhaps something much nearer to the epic Wordsworth himself will write; though the context will be quite different, the *Prelude* too will be an epic of an inner spiritual journey. And like Milton's Adam, Wordsworth had to absorb the wars and the violence – in Wordsworth's case, the French Revolution – and yet keep alive within his head a personal spiritual integrity. Adam rejoices at 'those coloured streaks in heaven', and he loves them for their meaning. That meaning of promise, and the sadness, courage and impressiveness of Book XI, lie somewhere behind Wordsworth's lines written a few weeks after this reading of Milton:

> My heart leaps up when I behold
> A Rainbow in the sky.

BOOK XII

MILTON HAS NOT yet finished with Adam's – and Eve's –
preparation for mortal life. The archangel Michael continues
his revelation to Adam of the future: the sequence of visions
in Book XI gives way in Book XII to a narrative account, almost at times a summary, of events through a massive sweep of
years. This is punctuated by Adam's interpretations and by his
gratitude to Michael 'sent from heaven, / Enlightener of my
darkness' (270–71).

The 'world destroyed' at the Flood gives way to the 'world
restored' (3) of the new society on earth and there is a hint of
the same romantic hope that we find altering the course of
Shakespeare's late plays: 'Thou metst with things dying, I with
things new-born' (*The Winter's Tale*). But history is not romance,
and soon enough, despite the fresh start and the pious peace of
'families and tribes / Under paternal rule' (23–4), one

> shall rise
> Of proud ambitious heart, who not content
> With fair equality, fraternal state,
> Will arrogate dominion undeserved
> Over his brethren, and quite dispossess
> Concord and law of nature from the earth,
> Hunting (and men not beasts shall be his game)
> With war and hostile snare such as refuse
> Subjection to his empire tyrannous:
> A mighty hunter thence he shall be styled
> Before the Lord, as in despite of heaven,
> Or from heaven claiming second sovereignty …
>
> (XII, 24–35)

This 'mighty hunter', rejecting such republican virtues as 'fair equality, fraternal state', is Adam's distant descendant, Nimrod, declared by Milton, and generally assumed to be 'the first king, and the beginning of his kingdom was Babel' (*Eikonoklastes*, 1649). The archangel Michael describes the building of 'A city and a tower, whose top may reach to heaven' (44). The builder's aspiration is for more than the 'subjection' of men ' to his empire tyrannous'; Adam realises that 'to God his tower intends / Seige and defiance' (73–4). Nimrod, for Milton, becomes a type for all tyrannic rulers; and these included Satan, whose aspiration was to usurp God, and Charles I (and Charles II), bolstered by the Stuart belief in the Divine Right of Kings, and the conviction that a king was above the law, 'from heaven claiming second sovereignty' (35). God makes one of his rare interventions into history: he forestalls Nimrod and turns the Tower of Babel into ridicule with the confusion of languages. Adam is 'fatherly displeased' with Babel's builder,

> O execrable son so to aspire
> Above his brethren, to himself assuming
> Authority usurped, from God not given ... (XII, 64–6)

but Michael allows him no rope for such righteousness; he is himself to blame:

> Since thy original lapse, true liberty
> Is lost, which always with right reason dwells ... (XII, 83–4)

Adam's own experience must sadly endorse Michael's correction: right reason (the working of conscience), as Michael indicates, is inseparable from true liberty, freedom, and if reason is

> in man obscured, or not obeyed,
> Immediately inordinate desires
> And upstart passions catch the government
> From reason, and to servitude reduce
> Man till then free. (XII, 86–90)

Adam had known this state; after the Fall and the fever of 'play' with Eve he knew that

[198]

understanding ruled not, and the will
Heard not her lore, both in subjection now
To sensual appetite, who from beneath
Usurping over sovereign reason claimed
Superior sway ... (IX, 1127–31)

Michael points out clearly that when man

permits
Within himself unworthy powers to reign
Over free reason, God in judgment just
Subjects him from without to violent lords; (XII, 90–93)

Society, in other words, deserves the tyrants it gets. Milton, despairing of his own society, must have abandoned all hopes for constitutional change during the popular early years of Charles II's reign.

Michael's account of the world after the Flood is 'as the former world', still tending 'from bad to worse till God at last / Wearied' with 'iniquities' withdrew, and averted 'his holy eyes' (106–10); men were worshipping 'their own work in wood and stone / For gods!' (119–20). The archangel moves quickly through Old Testament history (Milton knowing that the merest reference would be enough for his readers): one man is chosen by God to move away from the general corruption,

he straight obeys,
Not knowing to what land, yet firm believes ... (XII, 126–7)

A descendant of Adam, this man of faith is like Adam in that he will found a nation 'in a land unknown' (134), and in that it will be from his seed, as also from Adam's, that the 'great deliverer' shall come. Michael begins now in his account to make use of biblical names and we move from 'faithful Abraham' at speed through Isaac and Jacob, the sojourn in Egypt, Joseph, the captivity of the chosen people, the murderous Pharaoh, Moses and Aaron, the plagues of Egypt, the crossing of the Red Sea, Mount Sinai and the Ten Commandments, the making and the carrying of the Tabernacle housing God's Covenant, and finally the winning of the land of Canaan 'Promised to Abraham and his seed'. The rest, says Michael,

> Were long to tell, how many battles fought,
> How many kings destroyed, and kingdoms won,
> Or how the sun shall in mid heaven stand still
> A day entire ... (XII, 261–4)

Adam interrupts,

> now first I find
> Mine eyes true opening, and my heart much eased,
> Erewhile perplexed with thoughts what would become
> Of me and all mankind; (XII, 273–6)

He worries however about 'so many and so various' the laws, 'so many laws argue so many sins' (283). Michael explains that 'Law can discover sin but not remove'; the 'shadowy expiations weak, / The blood of bulls and goats', will not be enough and the people may then

> conclude
> Some blood more precious must be paid for man,
> Just for unjust ... (XII, 290–4)

Thus, in the fullness of time there will be a turn from 'works of law to works of faith' (306), and meanwhile the judges of Israel make way for the kings, David gives place to Solomon, the great temple is built for the ark, the corrupt people are made captive in Babylon for seventy years and when the temple of Jerusalem is re-built

> among the priests dissension springs,
> Men who attend the altar, and should most
> Endeavour peace: their strife pollution brings ...
>
> (XII, 353–5)

The sceptre of Israel is lost 'to a stranger, that the true / Annointed king Messiah might be born' (358–9). Michael tells Adam about the star, the 'eastern sages', the 'simple shepherds, keeping watch by night' (365),

A virgin is his mother, but his sire
The power of the most high; he shall ascend
The throne hereditary, and bound his reign
With earth's wide bounds, his glory with the heavens.
(XII, 368–71)

Not surprisingly, at this presentation of Christ as a political figure and a manifestation of the power of God, Adam is eager for the fight with the serpent:

say where and when
Their fight, what stroke shall bruise the victor's heel.
(XII, 384–5)

Michael explains that the saviour will save,

Not by destroying Satan, but his works
In thee and in thy seed ... (XII, 394–5)

The battle will be in the heart of man. Christ will, out of love and obedience, undergo Crucifixion; he will be seized, slain and nailed, a just man like the just men who have so far punctuated the church's history, but one far more barbarously treated. This 'Godlike act', continues Michael,

Annuls thy doom, the death thou shouldst have died,
In sin forever lost from life; this act
Shall bruise the head of Satan, crush his strength ...
(XII, 427–30)

Faith is the ransom, faith 'not void of works' (427) will be the key. The Resurrection, the legacy to the disciples, the Ascension, and the glorious Apocalypse

When this world's dissolution shall be ripe ... (XII, 459)

are speeded into Adam's consciousness and the reader's recollection. The Son will come

to judge both quick and dead,
To judge the unfaithful dead, but to reward
His faithful, and receive them into bliss,

> Whether in heaven or earth, for then the earth
> Shall all be paradise, far happier place
> Than this of Eden, and far happier days. (XII, 460–5)

The archangel Michael pauses at the thought of this Millennium day, the day which will cut across the vicious pattern of decline that has been and will be history with its bleak and tragic repetition of conflict. Against the conflicts – and it was thought that the world would last about six thousand years – the few just men struggle constantly to keep faith. These two currents move simultaneously onwards to their separate ends, catastrophe or fulfilment. Adam is ecstatic; he has understood the force of sacrifice:

> O goodness infinite, goodness immense!
> That all this good of evil shall produce,
> And evil turn to good; more wonderful
> Than that which by creation first brought forth
> Light out of darkness! (XII, 469–73)

In a way, *Paradise Lost* could have ended here with Adam's supreme recognition – available to every Christian – that from evil 'all this good' can come. For the reader, Adam's words recall and demolish Satan's proud boast to Beelzebub as the fallen angels lay defeated on the burning lake,

> If then his providence
> Out of our evil seek to bring forth good,
> Our labour must be to pervert that end,
> And out of good still to find means of evil. (I, 162–5)

The Redemption seems more wonderful to Adam than the Creation, and he even wonders

> Whether I should repent me now of sin
> By me done and occasioned, or rejoice
> Much more, that much more good thereof shall spring,
> To God more glory, more good will to men
> From God, and over wrath grace shall abound.
> (XII, 474–8)

This is something to wonder about, the *felix culpa* of original sin, the Fortunate Fall that brings ambivalence and paradox to that first failure (and all subsequent failures) in goodness and obedience. Michael says nothing to this, Milton does not endorse it, though he leaves the sudden half-serious notion hovering in air. Adam himself thinks no more of it and moves on to ask further questions. He is still learning, the world has not reached Apocalypse, the poem cannot end yet. There is more suffering and evil, the unhappy result of the Fall, yet to explain to Adam.

The archangel responds to Adam's continuing questions about the aftermath of the Ascension; he outlines the courage of the Apostles, the Holy Spirit, the speaking in tongues, baptism, miracles; he tells Adam that the Apostles 'win / Great numbers of each nation ...' and at length,

> Their ministry performed, and race well run,
> Their doctrine and their story written left,
> They die; but in their room, as they forewarn,
> Wolves shall succeed for teachers, grievous wolves,
> Who all the sacred mysteries of heaven
> To their own vile advantages shall turn
> Of lucre and ambition ... (XII, 502–11)

The 'prowling wolf' that Satan was likened to before he bounded into Paradise (IV, 183–7), the 'grim wolf' that 'devours' of *Lycidas*, the 'hireling wolves' whose only 'gospel is their maw' of Milton's sonnet to 'Cromwell, our chief of men', all these crowd behind the corrupt teachers of the early church, and indeed of the church in later times; they are 'wolves ... grievous wolves' (508), the grievous wolves that St Paul himself foresaw who would 'enter in among you' 'after my departure' (Acts 20: 29). Milton deeply lamented the conflict of secular and spiritual within the church: the forcing 'on every conscience' of 'Spiritual laws by carnal power' (521–2); the seeking of clergy

> to avail themselves of names,
> Places and titles, and with these to join

Secular power, though feigning still to act
By spiritual ... (XII, 515–8)

the 'heavy persecution ... / On all who in the worship persevere / Of spirit and truth' (531–3); and 'the rest, far greater part', those who

deem in outward rites and specious forms
Religion satisfied ... (XII, 534–5)

It is not a cheering picture and Michael's concluding comment begins wearily,

so shall the world go on,
To good malignant, to bad men benign,
Under her own weight groaning ... (XII, 537–9)

Nevertheless, he continues to assert again that through the woman's seed vengeance to the wicked will happen, that the Son is 'saviour' and 'Lord', that Satan and his 'perverted world' will 'dissolve', that after the purging and refining fire, there will be

New heavens, new earth, ages of endless date
Founded in righteousness and peace and love
To bring forth fruits joy and eternal bliss. (XII, 549–51)

Michael's sentence is a long one and it rises to a climax of power as he envisages eternal bliss, even re-using positively that difficult word 'fruits', a word that reminds the reader of that still innocent moment before Satan arrived on earth when God 'bent down his eye' and saw "Our two first parents ... / ... in the happy garden placed / Reaping immortal fruits of joy and love' (III, 65–7). There will be happiness again, but after how long a delay and at what cost.

The one certain and good thing in the archangel Michael's depiction of the church is that the Apostles left 'Their doctrine and their story written' (506), and that this was truth, 'Left only in those written records pure' (513). Milton's attack upon the secular contamination of the spiritual was not directed solely against the Catholic Church; the Reformation produced much failure, but there was one aspect of Christianity in which the Reformation could not fail – the availability for the English of the Scriptures in English. Milton believed in the existence of God and in the truth of Scripture. He felt that

> Every believer has a right to interpret the Scriptures for himself, in as much as he has the Spirit for his guide, and the mind of Christ is in him.
>
> (*Treatise on Christian Doctrine*, begun 1655)

This is the essence of Protestantism. Milton has been writing the Protestant English epic to rival Dante's great epic of European Catholicism. The history in Books XI and XII of man's relation with God since the Fall, the story of the early Church moving right up to Milton's own time, has prepared Adam to stand on his own as a Protestant; no priest will mediate between Adam and his God, and by his own efforts, in the knowledge and love of God, he will work out his salvation. He no longer needs Michael; he himself puts into words the sum of what he has learnt. It will be for him as it now has to be for Milton: there can be no confidence in public virtue; only in private can virtue be real, and it is as an individual with the same spiritual armour as all other individuals that Adam speaks to Michael, his 'seer blest' (a phrase taken over by Wordsworth for the prophet of truth at the opposite extreme from the learned archangel, the baby of the 'Immortality Ode'), of his understanding and his hope:

> Greatly instructed I shall hence depart,
> Greatly in peace of thought, and have my fill
> Of knowledge, what this vessel can contain;
> Beyond which was my folly to aspire.
> Henceforth I learn, that to obey is best,
> And love with fear the only God, to walk
> As in his presence ...
>   with good
> Still overcoming evil, and by small

Accomplishing great things, by things deemed weak
Subverting worldly strong, and worldly wise
By simply meek; that suffering for truth's sake
Is fortitude to highest victory,
And to the faithful death the gate of life ... (XII, 557–71)

He ends by acknowledging the example and teaching of 'my redeemer'. Knowledge, Adam attests, has not been begrudged him, nor clearly will it be; Raphael and Michael have taught him in the best way – through questions and dialogue as well as discourse. The aspiring short-cut to knowledge, the plucking of the fruit, had been folly. God will henceforth be for Adam a presence, and Adam's sphere of action will be the continuous everyday small successes in goodness that constitute the strength of a Christian life. There are no big movements in history on Adam's horizon, no changing society, no public exploit, no glory: fortitude and highest victory are to be sought in suffering, not in arms; and death, the feared consequence of disobedience, will be an opening into the immortal life that Adam and Eve have lost as their first state on earth. Walking as in God's presence, Adam now fully understands, has nothing to do with place, and the power to defeat the worldly strong lies in 'things deemed weak'. This is a long way from the grandeurs and 'heroics' of Satan.

Michael is pleased with his pupil:

thou hast attained the sum
Of wisdom; hope no higher, though all the stars
Thou knew'st by name, and all the ethereal powers,
All secrets of the deep, all nature's works ... (XII, 575–8)

With some repetition and some new emphasis the archangel spells out for the last time the qualities which the Christian soul must have while moving on his arduous way to salvation:

add
Deeds to thy knowledge answerable, add faith,
Add virtue, patience, temperance, add love,
By name to come called Charity, the soul

Of all the rest: then wilt thou not be loath
To leave this Paradise, but shalt possess
A paradise within thee, happier far. (XII, 581–7)

These are the strong Protestant virtues. There is nothing about
religious observance, particular ritual, priesthood or ministry.
The 'paradise within' will be 'happier far' than the Paradise of
the external garden because it will be achieved by the individual's private and active spiritual co-operation with God and
the constant exercise of virtue. It will not be easy, but it will be
the only true reward. If paradise can be within the mind, so, we
are reminded, can be its opposite, for Michael's phrasing recalls
Satan's mood as he looked towards still innocent Eden:

> horror and doubt distract
> His troubled thoughts, and from the bottom stir
> The hell within him, for within him hell
> He brings, and round about him, nor from hell
> One step no more than from himself can fly
> By change of place ... (IV, 18–23)

But it is time to depart. Michael assures Adam that Eve, having had good dreams in her sleep (how different from the disturbing dream that Satan had given her), will be calm; he suggests that Adam tell her in due course what he now knows,

> Chiefly what may concern her faith to know ... (XII, 599)

that is, mankind's great deliverance 'by the woman's seed', and
he trusts that both 'may live, which will be many days'

> in one faith unanimous though sad,
> With cause for evils past, yet much more cheered
> With meditation on the happy end. (XII, 602–5)

That shared faith, single in spirit, 'unanimous', will combine
the two almost contradictory essentials for the Christian:
sadness 'for evils past', for the Fall and 'all our woe' that has
been and will continue to be its consequence; and a cheering faith through 'meditation on the happy end', the promise

and the Redemption. No one note can be sounded at the end of *Paradise Lost*; there is no stasis, but for the Christian, as for the Christian year, and indeed the seasonal year, only constant renewal and the fine balance between penitence for the dark loss, and faith in the bright promise. The archangel Michael has been at pains right through Books XI and XII to bring Adam – and the reader with him – to the discovery of this for himself.

The poem ends on the human level. Eve, already wakened, greets Adam calmly; she knows as much as Adam and firmly uses the verb 'to know'. There is no frantic seeking now after forbidden knowledge,

> Whence thou return'st, and whither went'st, I know;
> For God is also in sleep, and dreams advise … (XII, 610–11)

Through dream, through an inner spiritual experience, through intuition, through God, Eve has become certain of that same dual strand of the desolating and the joyful:

> though all by me is lost,
> Such favour I unworthy am vouchsafed,
> By me the promised seed shall all restore. (XII, 621–3)

Was Milton being a man of his time in protecting Eve from the violence and horrors that Adam witnessed in the visions, or was he suggesting that there is more than one way of reaching truth: Adam's way of question and explanation, and Eve's more subconscious way of instinct and feeling? She no longer needs her flowers and her garden; place no longer matters. Her trust is now, as Michael had suggested it should be (XI, 291–2), in her husband,

> but now lead on;
> In me is no delay; with thee to go,
> Is to stay here; without thee here to stay,
> Is to go hence unwilling; thou to me
> Art all things under heaven, all places thou,
> Who for my wilful crime art banished hence. (XII, 614–19)

'Lead then' (IX, 631), Eve had said to 'the wily adder' (IX, 625) before going with that strange and plausible creature to the tree of knowledge; how much more mature she seems now as she accepts Adam's lead, and declares her love for him in these poised and formally balanced half-lines that remind us of, though they do not repeat, her exquisite love-song, 'With thee conversing I forget all time', of Book IV (639–56). But,

> all in bright array
> The cherubim descended ... (XII, 627–8)

It is time to leave Paradise as the cherubim glide

> meteorous, as evening mist
> Risen from a river o'er the marish glides,
> And gathers ground fast at the labourer's heel
> Homeward returning. (XII, 629–32)

After the teaching, the theology, the doctrine and the abstractions we are at ease again with a simile from the country and the English world. It is evening in the simile, night coming on and the mist, like the cherubim relentlessly gliding, is to be feared, but then the labourer knows where he is going. Deception and danger balance the safety of home; Adam will be a labourer too and will have to steer carefully, taking care that no serpent bruise his heel, and he is even now a labourer going home, home to an unknown world that he will make his home. With the brandished sword of God blazing before the cherubim, 'Fierce as a comet', the cool paradisal clime begins to parch with 'torrid heat, / And vapour as the Lybian air adust',

> whereat
> In either hand the hastening angel caught
> Our lingering parents, and to the eastern gate
> Led them direct, and down the cliff as fast
> To the subjected plain; then disappeared.
> They looking back, all the eastern side beheld
> Of Paradise, so late their happy seat,
> Waved over by that flaming brand, the gate
> With dreadful faces thronged, and fiery arms ... (XII, 636–44)

The Archangel has left them and the fierce cherubim guarding Paradise mean to convey the reality of the judgment God has pronounced: Adam and Eve are excluded and expelled from 'their happy seat', the 'happy rural seat of various view' as it had seemed to be forever in Book IV (247).

> Some natural tears they dropped, but wiped them soon;
> The world was all before them, where to choose
> Their place of rest, and providence their guide:
> They hand in hand with wandering steps and slow,
> Through Eden took their solitary way. (XII, 645–9)

So the poem ends; Adam and Eve are ejected from one world but they are born into another that will be meaningful despite difficulty. Their tears are human tears, not, like Satan's in Book I, 'such as angels weep', and they wipe them soon; they have a world before them, and not just for labour, but as a place where they will find rest. They will both choose and be guided, since providence, a concomitant of faith, is with them. Hand in hand as we (and Satan too) had first seen them, they walk together in the companionship and trust of marriage, and within that companionship they have the knowledge that they are individuals, each of them solitary, responsible to the private conscience. They walk like children 'with wandering steps and slow' and their wandering now is not the wandering of error but the tentativeness of those who are in new circumstances, facing a new challenge. Bewildered and purposive, they are both elegists for the lost and pioneers into the new.

★

Milton has made a brilliant shot at justifying God's ways to men, and perhaps he succeeds most in that he has written so richly human a poem and one that seems to propose that experience has a good deal in it that is good, that goodness is real, that a world of innocence is ultimately uninhabitable, that the tragic ambiguity of the human animal is the condition of our lives. Paradox is everywhere; our sense of eternity is bound in with our sense of history, our sense of truth, with our delight in fiction; and all of it in Milton's poem is presided over by God – and Milton believed in God; it is presided over by God and by language in the poem we read now. We live in the poem in a magnificent and multifarious world, we pass through immense stretches of time, we inhabit rich and various emotions. The poem is about growing up, and the reader, as much as Adam and Eve, grows up and delights not only in the clarities of the poem but in its shifting language where darkness is excessive bright, service can be liberty, peace corrupts like war, a man sees or dreams he sees. Insecurity of language and ambiguity of meaning are part of the excitement of *Paradise Lost*. Its characters, including that of God, the ultimate thinker withdrawn from action, continually intrigue us: the filial Son as God's instrument, Adam and Eve as they come to be like us, individuals themselves, Lucifer as he descends into Satan, reduced to indignity, and falls out of the poem except as the unquenchable idea of evil; but outside the poem, and certainly inside it, he has not ceased to exert his fascination, his appeal changing as the egotistic ambitions of different generations find in him their own desires. Chaucer, long before Milton, expressed that same mixture of admiration, regret and inevitable moral condemnation as he contemplated the fall of Lucifer:

> O Lucifer! brightest of aungels alle,
> Now art thou Sathanas, thou maist nought twynne
> Out of miserie in which thou art falle.
>
> (*The Monk's Tale*)

There is no concluding paragraph to any discussion of *Paradise Lost*, no final judgment. Wordsworth began where Milton left off:

> The earth is all before me – with a heart
> Joyous, nor scared at its own liberty,
> I look about, and should the guide I chuse
> Be nothing better than a wandering cloud
> I cannot miss my way.
>
> (*Prelude*, 1805, I, 15–19)

[211]

For Adam and Eve at the end of *Paradise Lost* with the world 'all before' them, the tears, the uncertainty and the loneliness are painfully there alongside the growing freedom and hope; for Wordsworth, beginning his epic where Milton's ended, all is joy, a sense of liberty, and the confidence that 'I cannot miss my way': any 'grove' by any 'sweet stream' could be his home, for the earth (not the much larger and more terrifying 'world' of Milton) is 'all before' him, and on the earth Wordsworth has felt at home all his life. Nevertheless, despite this auspicious beginning, and his own Edenic 'much favoured' childhood, the losses came, and Wordsworth depicts in *The Prelude* how, like Milton, he was learning all the time to build up an inner world. The French Revolution failed Wordsworth as the English people and the Commonwealth failed Milton. Milton believed in the God outside himself, and Adam and Eve, like their creator, would rely in their uncertain future upon faith in that God and upon their constant struggle for the 'paradise within'. Milton believed in addition in his heavenly Muse, his celestial Light, who could

> Shine inward, and the mind through all her powers
> Irradiate. (III, 52–3)

He believed, in other words, in the power of poetry, and Wordsworth at the end of *The Prelude*, complicated and uncertain as he was about the biblical God, fully endorsed the creative power of the inner God. From the top of Mount Snowdon, gazing upon a shifting moonlit vista, he calls that power 'the soul, the imagination of the whole' (*Prelude, 1805*, XIII, 65). It is for this imagination that we read *Paradise Lost*; it is for this that we read *The Prelude*.